ASSOCIATION

LOCAL INDEPENDENT
BAPTIST CHURCHES IN
FELLOWSHIP AND MISSION

....

EDITED BY **RYAN KING**
& ANDREW KING

Grace
Publications

Grace Publications
www.gracepublications.co.uk

Copyright © 2021 by Ryan King and Andrew King

All rights reserved. No part of this publication may be reproduced, stored in a retrieval system or transmitted in any form or by any means, electronic, mechanical, photocopying, recording or otherwise, without the prior permission of the publisher or the Copyright Licensing Agency.

British Library Cataloguing in Publication Data
A record for this book is available
from the British Library

Scripture quotations taken from the Holy Bible, New International Version (Anglicised) Copyright © 1979, 1984, 2011 Biblica. Used by permission of Hodder & Stoughton Ltd, an Hachette UK company. All rights reserved. 'NIV' is a registered trademark of Biblica UK trademark number 1448790.

Scripture quotations taken from The Holy Bible, English Standard Version® (ESV®) Copyright © 2001 by Crossway, a publishing ministry of Good News Publishers. All rights reserved. ESV Text Edition: 2016

First published in Great Britain in 2021

Cover design by Pete Barnsley (CreativeHoot.com)

ISBN: 978-1-912154-35-7

Printed and bound in Great Britain
by Clays Ltd, Elcograf S.p.A.

Contents

Preface
James M. Renihan / 5

Introduction
Ryan King / 9

1
Biblical and Theological Case for Associations
Robert Strivens / 19

2
Brief History of Baptist Associations
Greg Tarr / 45

3
From MASBC to AGBC(SE)
Paul Smith / 69

4
UK Mission and Church Planting
Nigel Hoad & Barry King / 115

5
Overseas Associations
Leonardo De Chirico & Jaime D. Caballero / 141

6
Maintaining Strong Associations
John Benton / 173

Conclusion
Andrew King / 201

Preface

James M. Renihan

In the twentieth century, a self-identifying term entered the vocabulary of Baptist churches: 'independent'. Though there are notable exceptions, numerous congregations severed existing relationships with associations, describing themselves as Independent Baptist assemblies (note the upper case 'I'), indicating that they had no formal affiliation with other congregations or organisations. Similarly, new churches, planted with the same ethos, also regularly remained aloof from co-operative societies. Though cordial relations with other Christian congregations may have been present, these were simply expressions of friendship and brotherly love, carrying no overtones of official commitment. The independency of these assemblies provided a veneer of purity, as it allowed churches to maintain distance from perceived weaknesses or failures in others. For many, this was a badge of pride, a strong assertion of local church autonomy. In reality, it was separatism, though often practiced with a smile. The isolating effect of this form of independency at times produced adverse consequences in Christian congregations. The results have not been good. Isolated churches seldom maintain long-term health and vigor; often they become ingrown or idiosyncratic, or both, in doctrine and practice.

The twenty-first century has brought a reappraisal of many of the ideas and practices popularised in the previous decades, especially those which seemed at first blush to be useful but have instead failed to deliver promised benefits. Among these thoughtful re-examinations, we find a growing interest in retrieving the historic practice of Baptist associations. This book, *Association*, is a sample of that desire for recovery. Containing contributions from an international array of authors, it helpfully adds a unified voice to the call for churches to commit to working together in formal and structured ways. The benefits to be reaped are many! Without proposing a new law by making demands for Baptist churches to enter formal associations, it calls the leaders and members of these congregations to rethink their previous decisions. It is irenic and helpful.

The early Baptists and their close cousins, the Congregationalists, often (in an ironic usage) called *Independents* – without the nuances attached to the term in the twentieth century – recognised the importance of freedom from external control, whether at the hands of the Episcopalian system of the Church of England or the church courts of Presbyterianism. The fathers (if I may so call them) of these congregationally oriented movements smarted under the domination and impositions of those who held the reins of ecclesiastical power. They recognised that each church properly gathered, whether large or small, contained within itself, through Christ's presence and gifts, everything necessary to fulfill its tasks. Their independency never, however, argued that this should mean isolation from others, or that formal co-operation is outside the bounds permitted by Scripture. To the contrary, they argued that the Light of Nature, right reason, and Christian prudence, together with the definitive examples of inter-church fellowship and joint activity attested in the New Testament, provide a strong basis for formal structure and co-operation. Whether in the words of the revised version of the First London Confession (1646) that churches 'are to have counsel and help one of another ... as members of one body ... under Christ their head' (Article 47), or the 'holding communion together' language of the Second London Confession (Chapter 26.14 & 15), to its implementation everywhere that English-speaking Baptist churches appeared, the practice of joining together in association marked the movement. These are simple facts.

Association provides examples of the early history of Baptist associations of churches, offers an exegetical and theological argument for their recovery, honestly recognises the advances and declines in some fellowships of churches (and provides brief but helpful analysis of each), considers the varying needs in international cultures and suggests paths to walk in the future. As an example of ecclesiological retrieval, it is a helpful contribution to an important discussion. May the Lord bless this book and bring about a strengthening of Christ's cause in the churches as a result.

Introduction

Ryan King

Across the great narrative of Scripture it is abundantly clear that we were created to be co-operative creatures from the very beginning and that we are recreated in Christ into familial, congregational co-operation within and among local churches.

The books of the Law tell how the first humans were not created from isolation but from the Trinitarian communion of Father, Son, and Holy Spirit. God said, as recorded in Genesis 1:26, 'Let us make man in our image, after our likeness.' Nor were we created for isolation. God, having created the first man, said in Genesis 2:18,

'It is not good that the man should be alone; I will make him a helper fit for him.'

The prophets implicitly rule out isolation. They prayerfully confess the sins of the nation, thus Daniel prays, 'we have sinned' (Dan. 9:5). They do not only address individuals, but most often a larger corporate audience, or leaders who represent the whole. When Ezekiel prophesied during the Babylonian exile, he condemned the 'shepherds of Israel', noting their isolation in privilege – they have only looked after themselves, leaving God's people scattered, alone, hurt, and hungry. When Haggai prophesied after the exile, he noted the nation's isolation in misplaced priorities. Each person was seeking his own interests, the development and decoration of his own house, but not the dedication of the Lord's house. The rebuke was corporate. Repentance would be corporate.

The writings wisely advise, 'Whoever isolates himself seeks his own desire; he breaks out against all sound judgement' (Prov. 18:1). Ecclesiastes reframes the same principle more positively, 'Two are better than one ...' (Ecc. 4:9–12).

Carry these principles over from the books of the old covenant to those of the new. Jesus does not roam about preaching on his own. He has an inner circle of three men (Peter, James, and John), a core of twelve disciples (including these three men), and a larger group of men and especially women who follow them, host them, and help finance their ministry (Lk. 8:1-3). Jesus sends seventy-two people out to proclaim the good news of the kingdom of God (Lk. 10:1-20). He does not send them one-by-one, but two-by-two. Here we see forming an interpersonal model for partnership and co-operation that would take its fullest form in the post-resurrection new covenant Christian context.

This descriptive model for how Christian individuals should go about ministry in co-operation with other Christian individuals becomes more prescriptive as we get into the epistles. The biblical concept of the church is that of a spiritual building (1 Cor. 3:16), body (1 Cor. 12:27), and bride (Eph. 5:22-33). Bricks and mortar must combine to construct a building; bones and all the other bits must be joined together to create a body; a bride is a particular kind of body, and the word 'bride' implies that there is to be a marriage union with a groom at some point – each of these images depict relationships of partnership, co-operation, and a sense of mutual responsibility.

What should be true between Christian individuals must surely be true of relationships between churches. Sadly this is not always the case. Theologically, churches that isolate themselves might plead the independency of the local church – 'we are under the authority of Christ alone' – at the expense of interdependency, which says, 'we join others in being under the authority of Christ alone'. Practically, associational affiliation is shunned, and as a result gospel partnership, multi-church financial co-operation, and joint social action often suffer if they even exist.

The concept of healthy co-operative fellowship between like-minded churches is pervasive in the New Testament. Bear in mind that the letter to the Galatians was written not to one church, but to multiple churches (Gal. 1:2) so when the apostle Paul says, 'Bear one another's burdens and so fulfil the law of Christ' (Gal. 6:2), he does not only have in mind the members of a church within their own church, but churches helping other churches!

This co-operative bearing of other churches' burdens is supported by the example of New Testament churches in response to various needs and crises such as church planting (consider Paul's church planting ministry in Acts, and how it came about and was sustained), theological formulation and cross-cultural missional reflection (Acts 15), sharing gospel workers (Acts 18:28), economic relief (2 Cor. 8), missionary support (Phil. 1:5; 4:15-16), and spiritual encouragement (1 Thes. 1:7-10). There is then no biblical basis on which a church can or should isolate itself from others of the same faith and practice – quite the contrary.

One word for the sort of co-operation and partnership outlined above is 'association'. Association is joining together with other people or organisations as allies for a common purpose. An association is the formally structured expression of such purposeful mission. This book is itself a work of association. It was commissioned by a committee representing the Association of Grace Baptist Churches (South East) on the occasion of their 150th anniversary. It has two editors, who despite sharing a surname are unrelated and serve as pastors of different local churches, in the same association. It features the contributions of several authors, some from churches that are part of formally organised associations, some not. Chapters four and five even have two authors each, with different nationalities, church contexts, personal perspectives, and ministry philosophies. This volume's essays then demonstrate by their very collection – never-mind content – that association is the antithesis of individual isolation, and is not best seen in coalescing around rigidly narrow tertiary standards of cultural uniformity, but by co-operating from a shared doctrinal basis and core distinctives in Christ-centred, kingdom-building unity.

In the first chapter, Robert Strivens develops a biblical and theological framework for geographically local and doctrinally aligned associations of churches, making the case that while formally organised associations may not be clearly identified in Scripture, there is sufficient grounds to encourage them.

Some historical application of these biblical and theological principles is further explored in the second chapter by Greg Tarr, who shares helpful anecdotes of associational expression from Baptist history: Abingdon, Northamptonshire, and Philadelphia. This is not history for history's sake, but instead pursuant of healthier associational life today, even in the seemingly little things.

In chapter three, Paul Smith narrows the historical focus to England's Association of Grace Baptist Churches (South East), formerly the Metropolitan Association of

Strict Baptist Churches, whose 150th anniversary has occasioned this book. In it, he charts the highs and lows of associational life, from its more hyper-calvinistic and some might say schismatic past, to days of evangelistic urgency and theologically conservative voice, to decline, to increasing evangelical catholicity, arrested decline, and gospel advance in the Association of today. When association works, it results in church planting and revitalisation. Kingdom advance through local churches working together is not a thing of the past, but actively continues today.

Nigel Hoad and Barry King have a great deal of experience in this area and in chapter four they recount the fruit of effective associational partnership they have personally enjoyed within and between the AGBC(SE)'s Home Mission and Grace Baptist Partnership. This chapter demonstrates from lived experience the potential of associational partnership, and should lead us to pray for and actively pursue closer relationships to this end.

Leonardo De Chirico and Jaime D. Caballero contribute to a more global perspective on Baptist church associations, writing chapter five from their respective European (Italian) and Latin American

(Peruvian) perspectives. They helpfully approach the subject with the same scriptural grid and core questions, but unique contextual voices. We must listen to and learn from such voices if we will do association better in our own context, and do mission better in theirs.

To what end is all of this writing about association? As the confessions and critiques of this volume should make clear, it cannot simply be to celebrate an association's 150th anniversary! There are, after all, 150-year-old buildings that are useless, crumbling, and should be torn down, if they have not fallen down. Like any building that stands the test of time, we must not fall into complacency but maintain any association if it is to be strong and healthy. John Benton, an elder statesman in AGBC(SE) life, brings the book toward its conclusion by identifying keys and threats to healthy association and makes three suggestions for building associational life.

Andrew King, the current Association Secretary of the AGBC(SE), concludes the book by weaving together its main themes into priorities for the future of the AGBC(SE) and, indeed, any other associations that may benefit.

Churches do not healthily associate for the purpose of denomination, to create a kind of franchise, but for co-operation, to build a family. They do not associate under dictation, to give one person or board of people control, but to co-operate, because Christ already has control, and has given us together a commission. Associations are not formed out of isolation, in further isolation, but out of co-operation and into further co-operation, because in creation we are made from the triune communion of God, for communion with God and one another, and in recreation by Christ, we know that he has died to bring us to God and we can draw near to him, together, without any dividing walls of hostility.

Organic association and organised associations among local independent Baptist churches are not ends, but means to the end: that the Lord our God be exalted among the nations through the witness of our fellowship and mission.

1

Biblical and Theological Case for Associations

Robert Strivens

Baptists hold firmly to the principle of the independence of the local church. We believe that the Bible teaches that each local church is self-governing. A church is entirely free from the authority or jurisdiction of any other church body of any kind. No synod, no council of churches, no church court, no bishop, superintendent or gathering of ministers and no other church (however large) has the power to instruct a local church how to conduct itself or to make laws or rules with which a local church must comply. In this respect, Baptists differ from Presbyterians, Anglicans and Methodists – all of whom have a hierarchical system which gives certain church bodies some degree of authority over local churches – and are aligned with congregationalists, who also hold to local church independency.

This has led, sadly, to some Baptist churches becoming practically isolationist. Holding strongly to a biblical view of self-government, such churches wrongly conclude that they need have no serious relationships or connections of any kind with other churches. They do not help other churches, nor do they accept help from others. They do not seek to work with other churches for the common good, nor do they embark on joint projects with others for the furtherance of the gospel. Their ministers see little or nothing of other ministers and their congregations are virtually ignorant of the activities, or even the existence, of other congregations. Even a cursory glance at the book of Acts and the New Testament letters reveals a level of communication and relationship between local churches that should immediately put to shame such isolationism.

Happily, very many Baptists are not isolationist. The general pattern over recent decades, in Britain at least, has been for Baptists and Baptist churches to co-operate through a network of informal contacts and parachurch organisations. In the crucial fields of mission, pastoral training and church planting, Baptists work together through a variety of institutions to further the work of the gospel. Baptist ministers meet in fraternals and conferences in order to network and develop relationships that strengthen their ministries and provide help and encouragement. Larger Baptist churches may provide financial assistance and other resources to assist smaller churches in gospel work.

All this is good. I believe, though, that there is a vital missing factor in these informal and, often, unstructured approaches to co-operation among Baptists. This chapter will argue that Baptist churches work best when they form part of a formal, structured association of churches.[1] I do not argue here that Scripture absolutely requires every Baptist church to belong to such an association. Nor do I argue that the Bible expressly instructs each local church to join with others in formal association. I do believe, however, that a well structured, soundly organised association of churches is of inestimable benefit to the churches that belong to it, to the Christians who belong to those churches and to the cause of the gospel in the area that they serve. And I believe that enlightened reason, the practice of the New Testament churches and a biblical theology of the unity of the church together form a very strong argument for Baptist churches to join and have fellowship together in associations of that nature.

1. The 'reason of things'

The Welsh-born Baptist minister Samuel Jones, who pastored Lower Dublin Baptist Church in Pennepek, Pennsylvania for over fifty years until his death in 1814, summarised the principles that he believed applied to associations of churches in his *Treatise of Church Discipline*. The practice of associating is, he wrote 'recommended by the reason of things', as well as by 'the spirit of religion, and apostolic practice'.[2] Benjamin Griffith, also born in Wales, pastored the Montgomery Baptist Church in Montgomery, Pennsylvania from 1725 until his death in 1768; he wrote of how it is 'expedient that particular churches ... meet by their respective messengers or delegates' by way of association.[3] The 'reason of things' and expediency are not the basis alone on which to establish how churches are to organise themselves. These Baptist ministers recognised, however, that there are certain general principles governing the manner in which humans organise themselves that it is useful to consider, even in relation to the organisation of churches. Such principles are by no means definitive and must certainly give way before the teaching of Scripture, which is our only authority in this matter. Nevertheless, it may not be entirely unhelpful to note the following factors, drawn from 'the reason of things', as we begin to examine this subject.

Churches vary in the gifts and resources available to them. May it not make sense for them to find ways whereby a church that is strong in a particular area is able to help one or more that are weak?

Churches share a common mission that is intended to cover the entire globe. Is there not something to be said for the idea that they should find ways of working together to accomplish this goal, particularly between churches that share a common theology and ethos?

Many different kinds of Christian church over the centuries – Presbyterians, Anglicans, Methodists and others – have operated on a connectional basis, whereby individual local churches are part of a larger organisation, structured in a formal manner. Such organisations have certainly proved beneficial to the churches concerned, at least in some respects. Should Baptists not consider whether the advantages that such organisation bring could be retained, without adopting the hierarchical approach which generally characterises such institutions or jeopardises the principle of the independence of the local church?

Past generations of Baptists often formed formal associations, at both regional and national levels, in order to help one another in the work of the gospel and to present to the society in which they lived a united testimony to Christ. Many of them believed that they were under a biblical obligation to do so. Should Baptists today not consider whether their forebears in the faith were not correct in holding this view? Is it not possible that we have lost something valuable, if we fail to follow them in this?

The attitude which calvinistic Baptists of the seventeenth century held towards the forming of associations can be seen from the confessions of faith that they agreed between themselves. Their views are encapsulated in the Second London Baptist Confession of Faith, agreed and printed in 1677 and reconfirmed at the general assembly held in 1689. Chapter 26.14 of that confession provides that churches 'ought to hold communion amongst themselves for their peace, increase of love, and mutual edification'. James Renihan has argued persuasively that, for the Baptists of the seventeenth century, 'communion' in this provision of the confession meant more than simply an informal network of churches enjoying fellowship together and engaging with one another from time to time. He has examined the use of that term in other Baptist writings of the time and in their associational records and related documents and has concluded that the word is used in those contexts in the strong sense of a formal, structured association of churches.

Those early Baptists believed that they were under a biblical obligation to meet in formal association for their common good, 'an organic union of persons united by common religious faith and rites ... the organized body professing one faith'.[4] The Baptist historian Ernest Payne argued that for the early particular Baptists, a local church:

> must be in communion with other local churches. That is an essential part of its churchmanship ... Associations, Synods, Unions and Assemblies of churches are not to be regarded as optional and secondary. They are the necessary expression of Christian fellowship, a necessary manifestation of the church visible. The local congregation is not truly a church if it lives an entirely separate life.[5]

Baptist churches of past generations, for all their belief in the independency of the local church, believed that they ought to be joined together in formal associations, for mutual assistance and for the sake of the gospel.[5]

These factors are historical and circumstantial. They look at what others do and have done and show that many Christians, of past and current generations, have belonged to churches that have in turn belonged to a wider, formally structured organisation of one kind or another. They demonstrate that even Baptists have, in times past at least, taken the firm view that they too should be part of a formal association larger than just the local church, albeit while preserving local church autonomy. These factors should at least make us ask the question whether we too, as twenty-first century Baptists, should not be committed to forming, or joining, formal associations of Baptist churches, as part of the mandate that Christ has given to his churches on this earth. It is right, accordingly, that we should consider this question seriously from the Scriptures.

2. What do the Scriptures say?

The Bible contains no express and direct instruction to churches to form themselves into associations.

The Bible also contains no express, direct instruction to Christians to join the formal membership of a local church. There is in the Bible no express, direct statement of the doctrine of the Trinity, as it has come to be expressed in western theology, nor is there any such statement on the hypostatic union. The Bible nowhere states in terms, 'The Holy Spirit is God', nor does it use the expression 'omnipresent' in relation to God. The Bible, nevertheless, undoubtedly teaches that Christian believers should commit themselves to a particular local church in a manner that approximates to what we would regard as formal membership. It also teaches very clearly that God is triune; that the deity and humanity of Christ are joined in a hypostatic union; that the Holy Spirit is God and that God is omnipresent. We hold to many fundamental, vital truths taught in the Bible, using terms and expressions that the Bible itself does not use. This is simply a function of how language works, as well as of the manner in which theological debate has developed over the centuries to define and defend biblical truth.

The point can be illustrated as follows, in the case of church membership. The New Testament clearly requires churches to maintain some kind of membership system: in order to exercise the kind of church discipline which the New Testament envisages, it is necessary to know who belongs to a particular local church and has thus brought themselves under the authority of that church. For that reason, some such system is necessary (1 Cor. 5:1-12; 1 Pet. 5:1-4; Acts 20:29-30); biblical teaching implicitly requires this, even though the New Testament does not expressly spell out that requirement in so many words. The New Testament instruction to Christians to recognise and obey the elders of the local church also implies that these Christians have an established, formal relationship of some kind to their local church (1 Tim. 5:17; Heb. 13:17).

A similar case can be made, I believe, for associations of churches – not that they have to be called associations or that they necessarily mirror precisely the form of the early particular Baptist associations, but that, in some manner or other, there ought generally to exist among local churches a structured bond between individual churches whereby they act together in certain defined areas. I will seek in this section to make this case by examining examples in the New Testament where churches engaged with one another or acted together. Example does not necessarily amount to obligation:

in the book of Acts, for example, not everything that churches are said to have done is to be imitated by every church since that time. It is surely right, nevertheless, to see how the New Testament churches behaved, as they were under the direct oversight and instruction of the apostles themselves, and consider whether and how we should seek to emulate them today. This was the approach to the issue that previous generations of Baptists took; to save reinventing the wheel, we will proceed by considering the texts that in their view constrained them to form and meet in associations.

There are, first of all, plenty of examples in the New Testament where churches are treated together, in one way or another. Paul wrote of how he had been personally unknown to the 'churches of Judea' (Gal. 1:22). He wrote to 'the churches' of Galatia (Gal. 1:2); Christ wrote to the seven 'churches' of Asia (Rev. 1:11); the Colossian church were to share their letter with the church at Laodicea and vice versa (Col. 4:16).

The high level of communication between the churches of the New Testament is impressive. It is clear that, even in those pre-digital days and before the existence of any organised postal system, churches in Italy, Achaia, Asia and the eastern Mediterranean kept one another regularly informed of their activities and of their needs and that messengers travelled often between them. Named individuals at the church in, probably, Corinth sent their greetings via Paul when the latter wrote to the church in Rome (Rom. 16:16, 21-23); the Philippian church sent Epaphroditus to Paul in prison in, probably, Rome, when they heard of his needs (Phil. 2:25-30); and there are many other examples of a similar kind (see, for example, Acts 14:26-28; 15:3-4; 21:17-19; 1 Cor. 16:19-20; Phil. 4:21-22; Col. 4:7-15; Heb. 13:24; 1 Pet. 5:13; 2 Jn. 13; 3 Jn. 15). The New Testament churches communicated extraordinarily well among themselves; they knew one another's circumstances and needs, joys and sorrows.

Not only did they share apostolic correspondence and communicate well with one another, churches in the New Testament provided practical help to other churches that were in need. In particular, there seems to have been an almost constant movement of preachers and other helpers in the work of the gospel between the churches of the New Testament, for their mutual instruction, encouragement and practical help (Acts 11:19-30; 15:32-33; 21:10; Rom. 16:1-2; 1 Cor. 16:10-12, 17-18; 2 Cor. 8:16-19; Phil. 2:25-30; 4:10-18; 3 Jn. 5-8).

The New Testament churches looked out for one another from a financial perspective too. Money was collected and given to churches in need, notably the church in Jerusalem (Acts 11:27-30; Gal. 2:10; 1 Cor. 16:1-4; 2 Cor. 8-9; Rom. 15:25-29). It is particularly remarkable, in this connection, that Paul described an unnamed brother as having been 'chosen by the churches' to go with him as he took and administered the money collected from the churches (2 Cor. 8:19). One cannot help wondering what process was adopted for 'the churches' to have made, collectively, this important decision.

One of the principal passages referred to by earlier generations of Baptists to justify the formation of associations was the meeting held at Jerusalem, described in Acts 15. The records of the Abingdon Association for 8 October 1652, for example, refer to this chapter as the basis on which churches should confer together for mutual advice on difficult questions, as it shows, they said, 'that the church at Jerusalem held communion with the church at Antioch, affording help to them as they could'.[6] Acts 15 is also one of the chief passages from which Presbyterians (and others who adhere to a more hierarchical mode of church government) argue for their system of church courts, assemblies and synods, with authority to adopt measures that are binding on local churches. This should not prevent us as Baptists from seeing here, at the very least, a New Testament example of two (or maybe more) churches consulting together, via representatives, in order to reach a common conclusion on an important question of doctrine: precisely one of the purposes for which Baptist churches have historically met in association.

No one of these texts on its own clinches the argument, but the sheer weight of the passages and texts which describe engagement of various kinds between the churches of the New Testament, despite all the disadvantages of modes of communication from which they suffered in comparison with us, should cause us to pause and question the relatively isolationist manner in which many of our churches today tend to behave. The frequency with which some kind of contact between different churches of the New Testament is mentioned, coupled with their acting together for certain specific purposes (in many respects similar to those for which the early Baptists associated together) and the strong impression that, in some sense, the churches of the New Testament viewed themselves as accountable to one another; the sense that they had of belonging to one another, such that they should help each other where they can – and do so jointly where that was practicable and useful; and the interest that they had in one another, such that they wanted to keep each other informed of their respective affairs and, where necessary, to meet to try to resolve the controversies and differences which arise in church life; all these factors together seem to indicate a strong, regular, deeply-held and valued mutual commitment among the churches of the New Testament, such as is not necessarily seen among Baptist churches of the twenty-first century.

3. Theology

But there is still more that can and needs to be said. The subject needs to be examined, not simply from individual texts and passages of Scripture, instructive as those are, but from the whole teaching of the Bible on the nature of the church – in other words, theologically. All Christians believe that there is, ultimately, one church universal of which Jesus Christ is the head. The question is, should the oneness of the church be expressed visibly in any form and, if so, in what form? This is a question to which John Owen gave some thought in the seventeenth century, particularly in his treatise *The True Nature of a Gospel Church,* published in 1689. Although Owen was then a congregationlist, his views on church government were influential on the Baptists of his day. Owen was quite clear that there was an obligation on individual churches to find means of expressing the unity of the church in some concrete form and he adduced a number of inter-connected arguments in support of his proposition.

The church universal and the local church

Firstly, he argued from the relationship between the church universal and individual local churches. He wrote, 'true gospel churches ought to hold communion among themselves, or with each other, as unto all the ends of their institution and order, for these are the same in all'. The objective of the church universal was 'the edification of the body of Christ in general'; the means by which that edification is to be achieved is, he said, 'committed jointly and severally unto all *particular churches*'. Therefore, he continued, it must be the case that individual churches need to act together, in order to fulfil the overall objective of the church universal: 'they are obliged unto mutual communion among themselves;

which is their consent, endeavour, and conjunction, in and for the promotion of the edification of the catholic church, and therein their own, as they are parts and members of it'.[7]

The post-apostolic age

Secondly, Owen argued from the fact that we live in a post-apostolic age. In the New Testament, it is the apostles, particularly Paul, who directed the churches, including the joint efforts of the churches to help and benefit one another. However, there are apostles no longer. Thus the only way of 'supplying churches' defects', as Owen put it, after the death of the apostles is by 'the equal communion of churches among themselves'. Christ has deliberately arranged that no church on its own is able 'always and in all instances to attain all the ends for which they are appointed, with respect unto the edification of the church catholic'. This is so that, just as they are all activated and bound in union by one spirit, they may be compelled to use their gifts and graces for the good of all. So it is that:

> the mutual communion of particular churches amongst themselves, in an equality of power and order, though not of gifts and usefulness, is the only way appointed by our Lord

> Jesus Christ, after the death of the apostles, for the attaining the general end of all particular churches, which is the edification of the church catholic, in faith, love, and peace.

Practical realities of geography and ease of communication restrict the actual exercise of this duty, but even so 'all places being made pervious by navigation', it is not impossible for some visible evidence of worldwide communion to exist. This is the only true catholicism.[8]

The union of the churches in Jesus Christ

Thirdly, Owen argued from the union of all true churches in the Lord Jesus Christ. The true bond of union between particular churches is not the Pope or the hierarchy or order of an established church, but:

> that they have all one and the same God and Father, one Lord Jesus Christ, one faith and one doctrine of faith, one hope of their calling, or the promised inheritance, one regeneration, one baptism, one bread and wine, and are united unto God and Christ in one Spirit, through the bond of faith and love.[9]

Christ is the head and fount of this union (Eph. 4:15-16; Col. 2:19; 2 Thess. 1:1). The bond of this union is the Holy

Spirit, acting in them 'by faith and love'. 'This is the kingly, royal, beautiful union of the church: Christ, as the only head of influence and rule, bringing it into a relation unto himself as his body, communicating of his Spirit unto it, governing it by the law of his word, enabling it unto all the duties of faith, love, and holiness.'[10]

This union is expressed, firstly, in a common faith by the profession of a common doctrine in the essentials. It is also expressed in a common practice – that of prayer – and in the administration of the sacraments. All profess a subjection to Christ and his laws. These together express the true communion of the churches. It is, for Owen, clear that such communion is meaningless if it is not expressed in the reality of the lives of the individual churches which are so bound together.

Owen is clear, however, that the means whereby this union is to be expressed is not outward acts of ritual or through hierarchies. The outward acts of mutual communion which evidence the spiritual union of the churches consist, argued Owen, in advice and assistance. Advice is provided through 'the meetings of divers churches by their messengers or delegates, to consult and determine of such things as are of common concernment unto them all by virtue of this communion which is exercised in them'. The need and basis for actual meetings arise from the light of nature and from the union which churches enjoy, so that 'none of them is or can be complete absolutely without a joint acting with other members of the same body unto the common good of the whole, as occasion doth require', which can take place 'no otherwise but by common advice and counsel', which has to involve 'convention in synods by their messengers and delegates'.[11] In other words, letters alone are insufficient; actual conference, as in Acts 15, is necessary.

Synods, or assemblies, of churches are therefore to be organised so as to concern themselves with:

- doctrinal matters and the profession of their faith;
- disturbances of the '*order, peace,* and *unity*' of the churches;
- maladministration of discipline;[12]
- and the worship and manner of life in individual churches.

The synod, or assembly, has no power, argued Owen, to instruct local churches to behave in a particular manner or to take or refrain from taking particular action – the local church is in no way subject to the binding authority of the assembly. The assembly does, however, have power to discuss matters such as those just listed and to render advice, as well as to withhold communion in appropriate cases from a church. These objectives were among those adhered to by the early particular Baptists for their associations. Owen's arguments lead to the conclusion that the tendency of Baptists today to place all their emphasis upon the independence of the local church and to relegate inter-church relationships to the optional is a serious ecclesiological deficiency. Reformation in this vital area seems essential. What then should be done?

4. Practical consequences

This chapter has argued that independent local churches must at all costs avoid isolationism and that they should seek to enjoy close relationships with one another in some formal and structured manner, particularly with those that are near geographically as well as theologically. This is clear from the 'reason of things', from the manner in which the churches of the New Testament related to one another and from the theology of the unity of the one church of Jesus Christ.

These various arguments together indicate that local churches are well advised to seek together to find means whereby they can together express:

- a genuine, living relationship between churches;
- which facilitates regular discussion of questions of mutual concern;
- and which enables co-ordinated action over a sustained period of time;
- covering not just one or two areas of mutual interest, but (at least potentially) all aspects of church life.

In particular this enables the churches to reflect New Testament practice by:

- providing advice in difficult questions and controversies affecting one or other church;
- helping churches in financial difficulties;
- supplying preachers for churches in need;
- carrying on gospel work jointly, for example in church planting;
- watching over each other in doctrinal matters;

- exercising love and fellowship as members of the one body of Jesus Christ.[13]

How is this to be achieved? As already mentioned, there are today a multitude of different ways in which independent churches co-operate, meet and work together. In England, these include the Fellowship of Independent Evangelical Churches, the various Gospel Partnerships up and down the land and associations of Grace Baptist Churches, as well as organisations such as Grace Baptist Mission, Grace Baptist Partnership, London Seminary, local fraternals, ministers' conferences and the like. To what extent, however, do any of these adequately fulfil all the ways in which we see the churches of the New Testament communicating and working together, as well as responding properly to the theological arguments that John Owen drew from the doctrine of the unity of Christ's church? What is the best medium through which local independent Baptist churches should seek to satisfy the criteria for mutual co-operation and joint action set out above?

It might be possible to cover all these matters through a range of different organisations, each committed to a different objective. It might be possible to address at least some of these concerns through merely informal contacts and relationships between churches. But it seems unlikely that such methods have the strength of structure and staying power necessary to fulfil all these purposes over a sustained period of time. The best approach, it is argued, is that initiated by the Baptist churches of the seventeenth century and continued by many in the eighteenth century – the formation of formal, structured associations, with a written constitution, a clear theological basis and regular meetings. Such organisations bring their own challenges: they can become overly centralised, or too bureaucratic, they can be overwhelmed by controversy or they can suffer from neglect due to apathy. No solution is proof against all forms of human sin and weakness. Yet formal associations of Baptist churches, properly constituted and wisely run, seem to be the best means of reflecting the range and depth of fellowship that the churches of the New Testament enjoyed among themselves, as well as the unity that they share in the Lord Jesus Christ. Such associations are heartily commended to the reformed Baptist community of our day.

Notes

1. This chapter is based partly on a paper first delivered at the Carey Ministers' Conference in January 2018.
2. Samuel Jones, *Treatise of Church Discipline* (Lexington, 1805), Chapter XII, 'Of an Association', point 2. My thanks to James M. Renihan for this reference and that in the following note. For Jones, see Horatio Gates Jones, *Historical Sketch of Lower Dublin (or Pennepek) Baptist Church* (Morrisania, N. Y., 1869), pp. 24–5.
3. Benjamin Griffith, *A Short Treatise Concerning a True and Orderly Gospel Church* (Philadelphia, 1743), 'Of the Communion of Churches'. For Griffith and the Montgomery church, see Edward Mathews, *History of Montgomery Baptist Church* (A.K. Thomas, 1895), pp. 22–3.
4. James M. Renihan, *Edification and Beauty: The Practical Ecclesiology of the English Particular Baptists, 1675–1705* (Paternoster, 2008), pp. 156–73, 183.
5. E.A. Payne, *The Fellowship of Believers: Baptist Thought and Practice Yesterday and Today* (Kingsgate Press, 1952), pp. 26–7.
6. B.R. White, ed., *Association Records of the Particular Baptists of England, Wales and Ireland to 1660*, Part 3, The Abingdon Association (Baptist Historical Society, 1974), p. 127.
7. John Owen, *Works*, Vol. 16 (Banner of Truth, 1968), p. 183.
8. Owen, *Works*, Vol. 16, pp. 184–185.
9. Owen, *Works*, Vol. 16, p. 189.
10. Owen, *Works*, Vol. 16, p. 190.
11. Owen, *Works*, Vol. 16, p. 195.
12. This point is noteworthy in the light of recent scandals; Philip Nye and Thomas Goodwin point out in their preface to John Cotton's, *The Keyes of the Kingdom* (1644) that abuse of power by church leaders is one leading factor argued by Cotton to justify the formation of associations. See, Larzer Ziff, ed., *John Cotton on*

the Churches of New England (Belknap Press, 1968), p. 75.
13. These points reflect the objectives of the Midland Association of particular Baptist churches, as agreed at its general meeting held on 26 June 1655. See, White, *Association Records*, Part 1, South Wales and the Midlands (Baptist Historical Society, 1971), p. 21.

2

Brief History of Baptist Associations

Greg Tarr

For many members of Baptist churches in the United Kingdom, the association that the church is part of is not a crucial aspect of their church life. Baptist associations can seem out-of-date, abstract, obscure, and irrelevant. Others are concerned that associations compromise the independency of the local church and are naturally suspicious of what appears to be an outside authority structure. After all, Baptists in England broke from the state church partly because they rejected the presence of ecclesial bodies standing above the local body of believers.

The aim of this chapter is to demonstrate that Baptist associations have proven themselves to be of vital importance throughout the history of the particular Baptist tradition.[1] The focus will mostly be on associations within England, but there will be a brief look at a major association within North America. It will quickly become evident that associations, when working well, have significantly enhanced the life of the local church, and have contributed dramatically to the spread of the gospel around the world. Far from being out-of-date, abstract, obscure, and irrelevant, I will argue that Baptist associations are essential, real, and tangible entities that can be meaningful for any member of a linked Baptist church. And I will show that, when they work properly, associations wholeheartedly affirm the independency of their constituent churches.

Historical summary

Before considering a few historical case studies, it is helpful to provide a summary of the kind of Baptist associations in view, where and how they started, and what the association landscape looks like today in the United Kingdom.

First, the subjects of this study are particular Baptist

associations, that is, associations of particular Baptist churches. The 'particular' refers to an understanding of Christ's death on the cross, and therefore the salvation of particular individuals. According to this view, also known as particular redemption, Jesus died only for the sake of those whom God has chosen.

Second, the associations started in England in the seventeenth century, with the Abingdon Association starting in 1652. An association in South Wales started in 1650, with one in the Midlands starting in 1655. Generally, there were small numbers of churches in each association, with three churches in Abingdon and South Wales, and six in the Midlands.

Third, the associations arose out of biblical convictions. The First London Confession of 1644 contained an article requiring churches to 'walk by one and the same rule and by all means convenient to have the counsel and help one of another in all needful affairs of the church as members of one body in the common faith under Christ as their only head'.[2] Many scriptural texts were cited to support this statement.

Fourth, several particular Baptist associations exist today as Grace Baptist associations. They include associations in East Anglia, West Anglia, and South East

England. These associations are much larger than those in the mid-seventeenth century, and so are frequently split into further geographic divisions.

Meeting of the Abingdon Association, 1652

Helping the weak

Paul's description of the church in 1 Corinthians 12 places a heavy emphasis on helping weaker members of the church. Using the analogy of a human body, Paul states that 'the parts of the body that seem to be weaker are indispensable' (1 Cor. 12:22). He goes on to say that 'If one member suffers, all suffer together' (1 Cor. 12:26). The application of these verses for local church life is clear and accords with Paul's instructions to the Ephesian elders, that 'by working hard in this way we must help the weak' (Acts 20:35). Churches are to be places where the members care for one another, and particularly where weak and struggling members receive help from those who are in a stronger position.

Baptist associations have historically taken this principle from Scripture and applied it to their own corporate life as a group of churches. Smaller, struggling churches have received help from larger, well-resourced churches. For most of 1 Corinthians 12, Paul is speaking about the local church, but he does make at least one reference to something bigger, when he says that 'in one Spirit we were all baptised into one body' (1 Cor. 12:13). The 'one body' here is not the local church but the worldwide, universal church. Therefore, it seems to be valid to take some of the imagery that Paul uses to talk about the local church and apply it to groups of churches, even though this was not the apostle's primary purpose. In several other places in the New Testament, Paul does explicitly promote and even command co-operation between churches.[3]

The inaugural meeting of the Abingdon Association enshrined some of these principles into the corporate life of the churches. The records show that churches in Henley, Reading, and Abingdon comprised the Association, and that representatives of these churches met together on 8 October 1652. They gave three reasons for the existence of the Association: to resolve doubtful matters and controversies, to give and receive financial help, and to uphold the principle described above, that members of the different churches are held together in relationships that go beyond their own church. They gave six pieces of scriptural evidence for this principle, of which the first is the most prominent.

They affirm the principle 'because there is the same relation between the particular churches each towards the other as there is between the particular members of one church'. The representatives conclude 'that every church ought to manifest its care over other churches as fellow members of the same body of Christ in general to rejoice and mourn with them'.[4]

Remaining pure

According to Gregg Allison, the church is pure both in a positional and a purposive sense.[5] Positionally, the church is already holy (1 Cor. 1:1-2), but purposively the church is to become 'holy and without blemish' (Eph. 5:27). In practice, Baptist churches attempt to maintain a converted membership and to exercise church discipline in cases of unrepentant sin. Every member thus plays a part in keeping the purity of the church intact, and many of the responsibilities of church membership concern the need for greater holiness and abstinence from sins that would bring the name of Christ into disrepute.

The members of the Abingdon Association saw that the same principles of purity that apply to churches also apply to associations. As with church membership, new churches that conformed to the doctrinal standard could be welcomed into the Association, but churches could also be removed if the purity of the Association had been compromised. Although it is a parallel with church discipline, this action was not discipline in the biblical sense, it was more of a sanction. According to the record of the October meeting, this was done 'to keep each other pure and to clear the profession of the gospel from scandal which cannot be done unless orderly walking churches be owned orderly and disorderly churches be orderly disowned'.[6] Notice the reason given for this practice, to avoid scandal. The sad reality is that a church that tolerates sin within its membership or that preaches a false gospel damages the corporate witness of the universal church, and so the name of Jesus is dishonoured. In removing a church, the association acts out of a zeal for God's glory in order to avoid a compromised witness.

This evangelistic thrust is evident later in the record of the October meeting. One of the purposes of the Association was 'to convince the world, for by this all men shall know by one mark that we are the true churches of Christ'.[7] This statement seems to allude to John 13:35, where Jesus, speaking of love between believers, says 'by this all people will know that you are my disciples'. The implication is that true churches, as well as being those that are marked by the preaching of the gospel, the ordinances, and church discipline, are also those that love other churches. And just as true love between individuals involves discipline (Heb. 12:5-11), so true love between churches can require a church to be removed from the association and welcomed back once corrective action has been taken.

Exciting general meetings

In my experience, the Annual General Meeting of a local Baptist association has not always captivated the hearts and minds of individual church members as much as it should. For many, the meetings do not hold interest for them to justify giving up time to travel to the meeting.[8]

I wonder if we could learn something from our Baptist forebears that might make these meetings more useful, and dare I say, more exciting, for church members. Recall, for instance, that part of the purpose of the Abingdon Association was to resolve doubtful matters and controversies. The way this worked is that representatives of the churches would meet to discuss questions that originated in the churches, and once they had reached a resolution, the decision would be communicated back to the churches. Examples of the issues that were covered include discerning genuine conversions and issues relating to marriage. The Association records cite the Jerusalem Council in Acts 15 as the scriptural warrant for this practice.

I think it would have been fascinating to have been present at the Jerusalem Council. It is not clear exactly who attended the meeting, but the evidence from the text points to a larger group than just the apostles and elders of the Jerusalem church.[9] At stake was one of the most contentious issues raised by the inclusion of the Gentiles in the plan of salvation, and there was no shortage of opinions on the subject! No doubt many speakers addressed the question, outlined the scriptural support for their position, and attempted to persuade the others. Notwithstanding the huge ramifications of the decision that needed resolving, it would have been both intellectually and theologically stimulating to have been in attendance.

While Christians in the United Kingdom do not face decisions of this magnitude today, there are still significant issues that face churches in our increasingly secular society. There are many 'doubtful matters' that need answering in a co-ordinated and collaborative way, and our associations are well placed to help answer them. Of course, individual church elder boards of larger churches could discuss and debate these issues internally, but that hardly follows the principle of helping the weak that our forebears advocated, nor does it ensure that all the churches achieve a common mind, walking orderly together by the same rule.

Conclusion

The Abingdon Association has much to teach church members about the importance and purpose of Baptist associations. Churches are to look out for each other by helping the weak, by remaining pure, and by addressing some of the most important issues of the day. One comment in the record of the October meeting summarises the purpose well, 'The work of God, wherein all churches are concerned together, may be more easily and prosperously carried on by a combination of prayers and endeavours.'[10] May God give our churches the humility to accept that his work goes beyond our four walls and the determination to work together with other like-minded churches for his greater glory!

Northamptonshire Association prayer call, 1784

The Northamptonshire Association was home to four of the giants of Baptist history: Andrew Fuller, John Sutcliff, John Ryland, Jr., and William Carey. The first meeting of the Association was held in 1765, but it was at a meeting in Nottingham in 1784 that Sutcliff proposed a call to prayer. The purpose of the prayer call, recorded in the 1784 Circular Letter of the Association, was that 'the Holy Spirit may be poured down on our ministers and churches, that sinners may be converted, the saints edified, the interest of religion revived, and the name of God glorified'.[11]

The prayer call involved the churches in the Association setting aside one hour on the first Monday evening of every month to pray for revival. Sutcliff wanted the churches to be praying at the same time if possible, and so various times were suggested depending on the time of year. The general expectation was that church members would travel to the church building to attend the prayer meeting, since the times of the meeting were set depending on the hours of daylight. However, if church members lived some distance from their church, they were encouraged to gather in smaller groups with those who lived nearby.

One of the fascinating hallmarks of this scheme was Sutcliff's willingness to involve other Christians from outside the Baptist tradition. He rightly recognised that God's plan to draw people from all nations to himself went beyond the boundaries of one denomination. He said, 'we shall rejoice if any other Christian societies of our own or other denominations will unite with us and do now invite them most cordially to join heart and hand in the attempt'.[12] But Sutcliff also recognised that Christians of all stripes were facing a common enemy, and unnecessary division only played into the devil's hand. He pleaded with Christians:

> There are but two parties in the world, each engaged in opposite causes; the cause of God and of Satan; of holiness and sin; of heaven and hell. The advancement of the one, and the downfall of the other, must appear exceedingly desirable to every real friend of God and man. If such in some respects entertain different sentiments, and practice distinguishing modes of worship, surely they may unite in the above business. O for thousands upon thousands, divided into small bands in their respective cities, towns, villages, and neighbourhood, all met at the same time, and in pursuit of one end, offering up their united prayers, like so many ascending clouds of incense before the Most High![13]

The prayer call had truly remarkable results, for within ten years, the modern missionary movement as we know it was formed. The Baptist Missionary Society was created in 1792 at a meeting in Kettering, attended by, among others, Fuller, Ryland, Sutcliff, and Carey. The BMS sent its first missionaries, William Carey and John Thomas, to India in 1793. Drawing on this, and many other examples in the history of the church, it is evident that prayer always precedes major revival and new works of God. T.S.H. Elwyn writes that the prayer call 'was one of the most decisive events in the life of Dissent in that period, and probably for all Christendom'.[14] Sutcliff and his contemporaries desperately wanted to see the gospel bearing fruit in their own land and across the world, and so they turned to prayer. We must do the same.

The ministers' fraternal of 1785

It is remarkably common to find different versions of the same event in history, and so part of the job of a historian is to weigh and analyse conflicting sources and to make a sound judgement based on the evidence available. In Baptist history, there is a well-known example of a disputed conversation that took place between William Carey and John Collett Ryland at a meeting of minsters associated with the Northamptonshire Baptist Association. Whether the alleged dialogue took place or not, it is instructive to use the account to consider the limitations of Baptist associations.

In modern evangelical thinking, it is taken for granted that it is incumbent upon Christians to share the gospel throughout all the world. However, in the eighteenth century, a form of calvinism had taken hold in England that required individuals to determine whether they were part of God's elect, rather than being assured of salvation on account of Christ's work on the cross and their profession of faith. Furthermore, this hyper-calvinism did not advocate the issuing of the gospel call. In response to this, pastors and theologians such as Andrew Fuller argued that the gospel should indeed be preached to everyone. Fuller taught that faith in Christ was a duty of the unconverted and pointed to several passages in Scripture that summoned the unbeliever to faith. Therefore, it was the responsibility of Christians to issue this call, and so participate in evangelism and mission.

It was in this context that William Carey presented a topic for discussion at the meeting of ministers in 1785. He suggested, referring to Matthew 28:19-20, that they discuss 'whether the command given to the apostles to "teach all nations" was not obligatory on all succeeding ministers to the end of the world, seeing that the accompanying promise was of equal extent'. John Collett Ryland is said to have responded by saying, 'Young man, sit down. When God pleases to convert the heathen, He will do it without your aid or mine.'[15] The dialogue is disputed by John Collett Ryland's son, but affirmed by others who were present at the meeting. It is impossible to know whether it was said, or indeed whether John Collett Ryland was himself a hyper-calvinist. Some claim that he was waiting for a fresh outpouring of the Holy Spirit that would confer gifts on the ministers, but even this was later acknowledged to be a serious mistake.[16]

What is indisputable is that William Carey wholeheartedly believed that it was his responsibility to preach the gospel to all nations, and a few years later, in 1792, the Baptist Missionary Society was formed. Carey himself left for India in 1793, pioneering the modern missionary movement, and reversing a dangerous historical trend towards complacency and inaction with respect to the Great Commission. If there was a hesitancy on the part of ministers in Northamptonshire, then clearly the Association had some limitations. Achieving unity at a meeting where some denied the necessity to take the gospel to the whole world would not be necessary or desirable. Baptist associations have many strengths, but they are not ultimate. William Carey's story shows that God always overrules to achieve his purposes. Thus, within a healthy association, there may well be times when an individual or even a whole church must go their own way to follow the will of God.

Baptist associations in North America

As the Baptist cause spread across the Atlantic, many notable associations were formed across North America. According to its website, 'the Philadelphia Baptist Association is the oldest continuous association of Baptist churches in the United States'.[17] It was founded in 1707 by five churches, and currently contains 124 churches. Naturally, Baptist associations in North America followed many of the principles found in the English associations of the eighteenth century, but one area in which they stand out is their willingness to oppose the sins of society. In accord with the material presented so far in this chapter, this is a practice I think that British Baptist associations could profitably adopt going forward.

A meeting of the Philadelphia Association was held

over several days in October 1789 at which a Lewis Richards opened the meeting by reading from John 8:36, 'if the Son, therefore, shall make you free, ye shall be free indeed'. This was a fitting text given one of the topics that was on the agenda the following day. The minutes record that the Association declared their:

> high approbation of the several societies in the United States and Europe, for the gradual abolition of the slavery of the Africans, and for guarding against their being detained or sent off as slaves, after having obtained their liberty; and do hereby recommend to the churches we represent to form similar societies, to become members thereof, and exert themselves to obtain this important object.[18]

Several points are noteworthy concerning this statement. First, it recognises that changes in society do not happen overnight, that gradual change may come about by persistent campaigning and political action. Second, it charges churches in the Association to take up the cause, even to the extent of forming their own societies, perhaps in the local area to petition local politicians. Third, it sets a clear goal to work towards, and implies that significant effort will be required to obtain it. But fourth, and most importantly, the churches in association together made a clear moral judgement, that slavery was wrong and had to be opposed. This took place seventy years before the American Civil War, and so there was much difficulty ahead, but it allowed Christians in the Philadelphia Baptist Association to stand together on this important issue. As other Baptist associations were formed in other parts of the United States, a desire to engage politically became engrained in the DNA of many associations.

I would like to think that if I had been present in one of the churches in the Philadelphia Baptist Association in 1789 that I would have fully embraced the campaign, alongside my responsibility to share the gospel with unbelievers and disciple fellow believers. However, it is easy in the twenty-first century to become disengaged from politics and to become apathetic to the many evils of our increasingly secular society. I often think, what can I do, as one man, to affect the inevitable decline of Christian values that has accelerated over the last few years. But perhaps I am asking the wrong question. Maybe the question should be, what can our associations do to speak out against these things, and how can they mobilise churches to join in a united opposition to the laws which are contrary to Scripture?

Baptists in the United Kingdom need to recapture our political engagement, but we must do so together in associations, not as isolated individuals. With much prayer, perhaps God will stem the tide of increasing secularism and recapture our society for Christ.

Concluding reflections

What are some of the lessons that we can learn from our Baptist forebears and their practice of associating together as outlined in this chapter? Let me suggest two ways in which our churches can put some of this thinking into practice.

First, drawing from the practice of the Abingdon Association, larger churches within an association have an obligation to assist the smaller churches, in the same way that a stronger church member provides help to a weaker one. I have been fortunate enough to have seen some of this happen in practice, and even to have participated in the kind of assistance that our Baptist forebears envisaged. For ten years, I was a member of a large Grace Baptist church in the south of England, and for most of that time, we informally and sporadically provided help to other churches in the association. But there came a point when we decided to offer more focused and consistent support. This took the form of members of the large church visiting the smaller churches for a Sunday morning service on a rotation, so that the smaller churches had visitors coming every week. In time, this led to relationships forming which in some cases led to offers of practical help and significant needs being met. For example, one of the churches was without a pianist, and so a lady from our church went there to play the piano on a regular basis. For my part, I went weekly to one of the churches to help with their children's group, and eventually developed a strong friendship with the pastor and his family that continues to this day. The testimony of everyone who got involved with this matched the unsourced words of Jesus, that 'It is more blessed to give than to receive' (Acts 20:35).

I am not saying that all churches need to have a scheme that exactly matches what we had, but it is surely incumbent on well-resourced churches to have a concern for smaller churches that expresses itself in practical ways. As church members, we would never renegade on our responsibility to fellow church members who are struggling and in need, and indeed many churches have explicit covenants which *mandate* their members to do just this.[19] It would be unthinkable to give up on a brother or sister who was going through financial hardship, marriage difficulty, or a period of spiritual stagnation. And yet, somehow, larger churches can either be completely deaf to the plight of smaller, struggling churches in their locality, or if not completely deaf, they can provide support for a time but then become inattentive as the burden carries on. There will always be questions to ask about dependence and self-sustainability, but perhaps our churches have been too quick to give up? Our Baptist forebears would chide us for this attitude.

Second, drawing from John Sutcliff's call to prayer, our churches should surely imitate this practice. I have been living in the United States for the last few years and my church is part of the Southern Baptist Convention (SBC), a large denomination of Baptist churches stretching across the whole country. It is by no means perfect, but a decade or so ago, I think Southern Baptists recaptured some of Sutcliff's vison. In 2009, the former SBC President Ronnie Floyd issued a similar prayer call that was named the Great Commission Resurgence. It did not include all the elements of Sutcliff's call, as it would be a challenge to co-ordinate anything across a network of over 50,000 churches, but the associations in the United Kingdom could easily replicate Sutcliff's call to prayer. Who will lead God's people in urgent prayer for the churches, for the nation, and for the spread of the gospel all over the world?

Notes

1. Particular Baptist stands in contrast to general Baptist. The two groups are differentiated by their views on the atonement, since particular Baptists believe that Christ died only for the elect.
2. Crosby, *History of the English Baptists*, Appendix 2, p. 23.
3. For example, financial support is mentioned in Romans 15:26, 1 Corinthians 16:1 and 2 Corinthians 8 – 9.
4. White, *Association Records of the Particular Baptists*, p. 126.
5. Allison, *Sojourners and Strangers*, p. 134.
6. White, *Association Records of the Particular Baptists*, p. 126.
7. White, *Association Records of the Particular Baptists*, p. 127.
8. I was, however, pleasantly shocked to hear that a local Baptist association in Asia holds their annual meetings in an entirely different country, and most of the members of each church travel! In a country in which Christians are persecuted, these believers strongly value the fellowship and unity that their association life brings.
9. For example, Luke records in Acts 15:2 that 'some of the others' travelled to Jerusalem with Paul and Barnabas. Maybe this included lay people from the church in Antioch? It is unlikely that the believers who rose up in verse 5 were elders or apostles since they 'belonged to the party of the Pharisees'. Luke records that 'all the assembly fell silent' in verse 12, suggesting again that a large group of people were present.

10. White, *Association Records of the Particular Baptists*, p. 126.
11. Elwyn, *The Northamptonshire Baptist Association*, pp. 15–7.
12. Haykin, *Ardent Love for Jesus*, p. 65.
13. John Sutcliff, 'Preface', 'An Humble Attempt to Promote Explicit Agreement and Visible Union of God's People in Extraordinary Prayer', *The Works of Jonathan Edwards*, Vol. 2.
14. Elwyn, *The Northamptonshire Baptist Association*, p. 18.
15. Stanley, *History of the Baptist Missionary Society*, pp. 6–7.
16. Murray, 'William Carey: Climbing the Rainbow', pp. 20–1.
17. See https://philadelphiabaptist.org/history (accessed 30/04/2021).
18. *Minutes of the Philadelphia Baptist Association*, p. 246–7.
19. My current church, Third Avenue Baptist in Louisville Kentucky, has a covenant which all members sign when they join. The covenant is recited every members' meeting and at the Lord's Supper. It has a clause which reads, 'That we will participate in each other's joys, and endeavour with tenderness and sympathy to bear each other's burdens and sorrows.' For the entire covenant, see, https://thirdavenue.org/s/3ABC-Church-Covenant.pdf (accessed 22/04/2021).

3

From MASBC to AGBC(SE): 150 Years of Association

Paul Smith

In Mayfair, in Mt Zion, Hill Street, messengers gathered for the 1877 AGM to celebrate the sixth anniversary of the Metropolitan Association of Strict Baptist Churches (MASBC). The president, J.S. Andersen, was thrilled to record that the MASBC had lived 'longer than any prior institution had lived. Poor churches had been helped by it, brethren had been encouraged and it was no small mercy to be able to say that the committee and the delegates in all the meetings held that day had shown a hearty good-will towards one another, and a Christian affection for each other.' If six years were a cause for

Victorian believers to rejoice, how much more so is the preservation of the Association for 150?

Phase I: Standing together (1871–1921)

The Association began at the high point of both empire and churches in England. William Gladstone was Prime Minister; Queen Victoria was at the heart of her reign. Spurgeon's Metropolitan Tabernacle had been open for a decade and William Booth had founded the Salvation Army seven years before. Stanley was getting ready to leave Zanzibar to find Livingstone. London was a melting pot of ideas. Strict Baptist congregations were 'migratory and fluctuating and changeable' with people even reading announcements in Christian periodicals to choose their preacher for that Sunday.[1]

Seeking fellowship

The MASBC was formed by churches who believed both in formal association and that such an association must have Strict Baptist distinctives. The London Baptist Association had been launched at the Metropolitan Tabernacle in 1865. However, although Strict Baptists were its biggest grouping, it made no issue of calvinism or communion.[2] The initial twenty-three associating churches of the MASBC felt 'a strong desire for closer union' with those fully like-minded.

Providing a positive alternative helped avoid a critical spirit. To cries of 'hear, hear!' at the 1877 AGM the president stated that 'he was thankful that the associated churches and ministers seemed quite agreed in their opinion as to the folly of spending time in abusing those who differed from them'. In 1873, J.T. Briscoe from Salem Chapel, Meard's Court, said that 'the churches had resembled the little pools left by the ebbing tide – separate from each other, with no channel of communication. The association had formed a channel, but they needed to be overflowed with divine influence.' (Unsurprisingly he was tasked with the Friday night lecture for young ministers on 'Illustrative preaching' the following year.)

There was ample opportunity for involvement. There was a March AGM and October half yearly meeting (HYM). From 1887 those seeking re-election had their committee attendance listed on the voting slip. Later, names were suggested for vice-president at the HYM before a vote to set up a two-man run-off at the AGM. A year as vice-president led to the next as president. Most business was mundane. Meetings had opening devotions, correspondence, applications for membership, preparation for half yearly or annual meetings and administration of various funds. MASBC numbers peaked in 1901 with sixty-seven churches and 4,253 members.

Controversy on hymnbooks is nothing new. In 1901 a proposal for a new hymnbook 'caused a very lively discussion', being defeated 41–39. After deciding it was necessary in 1907, responses from individual churches saw sixteen opposed to change and of the six churches in favour of a new hymnbook, only one was willing to adopt it!

Sharing funds

From its inception, the Association was shrewd in managing and strategic in deploying its funds. From 1872, funds for a new chapel required three-quarters already promised or raised and the chapel held in trust for the Strict Baptist denomination. The Loan Fund, proposed in 1874 was 'to assist in the erection, or liberation from debt, of the chapels or buildings of the Associated Churches and in acquiring freehold sites for the erection of such buildings by loans free of interest'. The term could be no more than ten years with quarterly repayments.

Soon church members were standing as security.

From 1875, the General Fund could be used compassionately to assist sick or disabled ministers or their widows. The Honorary Secretary appealed for extra help in MASBC's magazine, *The Gospel Herald* when, despite a drapery business, the widow of Pastor William Bracher of West Ham could not cover a £65 mortgage. By 1904 the funds stood at these levels (with rough modern equivalents stated):

Loan Fund – £4102 (£320,000)
General Fund – £307 (£24,000)
Pastors' Benevolent Fund – £618 (£48,000)
Sunday School Committee – £63 (£5,000)

Funds were carefully stewarded. The 1905 AGM decided that a pastor's widow couldn't access the benevolent fund should she remarry. In 1907 the Association incorporated as the Association of Strict Baptist Churches Limited (ASBCL). The lack of 'Metropolitan' was probably deliberate because ASBCL came to act as trustee for churches outside the MASBC area. Later in the twentieth century it also took on trusteeship for Baptist churches which were particular but not strict.

Standing on fundamentals

The Association endured the rise of liberalism by standing resolutely for what it believed. At the 1873 AGM, President Hazleton stated that 'They were not ashamed of the denomination to which they belonged; for he believed they were the only denomination who contended for the whole of "the faith once delivered to the saints."' They could meet with other denominations for general purposes, but for denominational purposes they must remain isolated: not that they had separated from others, but because others had separated from them. They had united as an association for the maintenance of the truth, and 'a three-fold cord was not easily broken'.

The central defining characteristic was communion. The first resolution of the opening meeting illustrates this: 'That an Association of Particular Baptist Churches, in and around London, holding Strict Communion principles, be formed and called, "The Metropolitan Association of Strict Baptist Churches."' There were other Baptist churches (like those in the Baptist Union) and there were other particular Baptist churches (like the Metropolitan Tabernacle). But the Association was of Strict Baptist churches.

The Association considered itself part of the Strict Baptist denomination. Within this grouping of churches its doctrinal basis was relatively broad. The twelfth clause in 1871 stated: 'The necessity of immersion on a profession of repentance and faith, in order to church fellowship and admission to the Lord's-table.' The MASBC held communion was only for biblically baptised church members, but many Strict Baptist churches welcomed only baptised members of churches of the 'same faith and order' i.e. Strict Baptists like them. Interestingly, Spurgeon did not just leave communion to the individual conscience. He required baptism and church membership for permanent communion but allowed temporary communion for paedobaptists for 'two or three months'.[3] In some ways, amongst particular Baptists, the MASBC held a position between Spurgeon and the Gospel Standard.

To avoid problems, the MASBC contained clear statements on their view of gospel preaching. Like a previous Strict Baptist association of seven churches,[4] the MASBC held to the 'duty of preaching the gospel to every creature'.[5] But was it the duty of every creature to believe? This issue had led one previous association to split in 1846 through disagreement[6] and another to peter out by 1855 despite – or perhaps because of – ambiguity on this point.[7]

At its inaugural meeting in 1871, the MASBC unanimously agreed 'that saving faith is not a legal duty but the sovereign and precious gift of God'. The founders rejected: 'duty faith' – those not chosen to receive the gift of faith did not have a duty to believe the gospel. In those early years, the man teaching young MASBC preachers – William Jeyes Styles (1842-1914) – was a firm opponent of duty faith. At the 1873 AGM he said 'the personal honour of the Holy Spirit' was at stake. Styles called Spurgeon, in whose Pastors' College he trained, 'our most beloved and esteemed friend' but he fiercely critiqued Spurgeon's open offer of the gospel.[8]

Styles drew an 'obvious distinction between preaching Faith declaratively to all men, and directly and personally to sensible sinners only'.[9] Styles said that preachers must declare that all who believe are pardoned, but only command belief to those 'pricked in their heart' (Acts 2:38). He preached gospel indicatives usually without gospel imperatives. Styles argued that 'duty-faith is denied by all Strict and Particular Baptists' demonstrating this by the MASBC's doctrinal basis, and that of the Strict Baptist Mission which preceded it.[10]

Thus, the MASBC was formed by those with clarity on the gospel but confusion on the gospel offer. This meant that in its churches 'the gospel was not offered, but it was clearly present: faith was not preached as a duty, but the need of it was never overlooked ... there was a genuine concern for Mission, for the salvation of souls at home and overseas'.[11]

However, the extent of hyper-calvinism varied even in those early days. Hazleton, who proposed the duty faith clause, is quoted as saying: 'feed my sheep, defines our commission. We are neither to form them nor find them'.[12] Styles contended on the issue because he feared drift towards an open gospel offer. Some MASBC churches were involved in evangelistic tract distribution. Pastor Robert Sears wrote a monthly *Life and Light* with gospel content from at least 1888 which had a monthly circulation of 10,000 by 1898, half distributed around his church.[13] Forty-two MASBC churches supported the Strict Baptism Mission by 1894-5.[14]

The MASBC stood strongly against liberalism and drift. At its half yearly meeting on 11 October 1887 there was a vote of sympathy with Spurgeon for his stand against doctrinal downgrade in *The Sword and Trowel*. Both president and secretary signed a motion forwarded to Spurgeon that the MASBC 'desires to express its sympathy with Mr C.H. Spurgeon in the position he has taken in defence of truth.' Spurgeon appreciated their support. In 1907 a resolution against 'the New Theology' – liberalism promoted by George Bernard Shaw – was 'heartily and unanimously carried'.

In 1888, the MASBC was alarmed by Queen Victoria's diplomatic relations with the papacy, including congratulating LEO XIII on the fiftieth anniversary of his ordination. A letter noted that she: 'solemnly and sincerely, in the PRESENCE OF GOD, professed, testified and declared that the Sacrifice of the Mass, as now used in the Church of Rome, is superstitious and idolatrous'. Therefore the MASBC 'Did hereby record our solemn and emphatic PROTEST before GOD against a policy calculated to endanger the security of the Throne ... and to dishonour the NAME of HIM by who kings reign'.

Spreading the faith

The Association was born when people were pouring into London from the countryside. Between 1801 and 1871 the population leapt from one to four million (half of its population today). The need for church planting was urgent. According to the 1851 census, 35% of the population of England and Wales attended church but only 21% of Londoners.[15] By 1903 almost 30% of Londoners attended a church.[16] Particular Baptist church attendance was rising. In the first half of the nineteenth century, the number of particular Baptist churches in London tripled to 120.[17] This more than matched the pace of population growth.[18]

The MASBC wanted Strict Baptist churches planted. It had two stated aims: 'to promote the unity, edification, and prosperity of the Churches' and then 'to devise and employ means for extending the Cause of God in London and its suburbs'. In 1877 the secretary stated that 'attention of the committee has been seriously directed to the necessity of establishing causes of our faith and order in the districts of the metropolis at present destitute'. The MASBC placed great importance in getting their message out, purchasing *The Gospel Herald* in 1880 which was amalgamated with *The Earthen Vessel* in 1887 – the year after the death of its editor, Charles Banks.[19]

Despite the duty faith clause there were clear gospel desires from the very start. The 1878 annual report understands the prayer 'thy kingdom come' to mean it is 'Jehovah's purpose to extend the kingdom of grace by gathering to his people from the ranks of the ungodly around us'. So, the MASBC should use 'all scriptural means within its power to spread abroad the knowledge of God and his soul-saving truth, that, under its influence, precious souls may be made to partake of like spiritual blessing with ourselves'. A man suitable for a pastorless church (of which they were too many) was one with 'compassion and pity' for those who 'are out of the way' and endowed with spiritual wisdom to 'win souls'.

Two decades later, the evening meeting at the 1903 AGM focussed on 'the need of an evangelistic spirit in our churches'. The AGM was, however, unwilling to approve the new Home Mission committee's recommendation to appoint (and fund) an evangelist. Yet in the Welsh revival year of 1904, October's half yearly meeting saw unanimous support for setting up a Home Mission with its own funds. Home Mission was to 'use its best endeavours to establish preaching stations in districts where, at present our denomination is unrepresented'. The committee felt that 'aggressive steps' were needed towards MASBC's aim of extending the cause of God. The Home Mission sub-committee therefore got to work 'educationally assisting young men ... to become active labourers in the Lord's work', asking weaker churches if they would receive a pastor to revive weekly evening services, and asking 'friends living in suburban districts' to open a way to conduct services.

State of the Association after fifty years

On the eve of war in 1914, there was consternation as the Soho church wanted to sell their chapel. The Association had been founded in Soho's previous chapel in Oxford Street. The church wanted to sell its cavernous 500-seat Shaftesbury Avenue chapel to move to Finchley (it is now High Road Baptist Church, Finchley). The MASBC committee (meeting in the chapel!) urged 'the moral rights of the Association to be considered in the matter, as much of the money had been asked for and given on the grounds of the building being available for Denominational meetings'. After sapping huge amounts of committee time, one-twentieth of the sale proceeds were given to the Pastoral Aid fund in 1917. Such disagreements were obviously distracting. At the 1918 AGM the president noted that 'want of unity of energy was sadly manifest and members were not yet ready to sink personal opinions for the good of the cause and the glory of God'.

If there were difficulties at Association level, there was energy at the new district level (N, SE, SW, E, W), launched in 1917. East District elected chair and secretary, agreed to avoid clashes of anniversaries and public meetings, and launched monthly prayer meetings plus four special prayer meetings for an outpouring of the Spirit. By 1927 SE and E districts had an 'Association Sunday' of pulpit exchanges. A young people's sub-committee recommended brightening Sunday school buildings and making 'them warm, comfortable and as home-like as possible in order that junior and senior scholars alike may feel pleasure and enjoyment in attending and that they may realise that the officers and teachers, and that also the Churches, take a real interest in both their spiritual and temporal welfare'.

The minute books give snapshots of life on the home front during the First World War. There was a united prayer meeting in September 1914. A letter to the King and Prime Minister the following month stated that 'prayer is a mighty force and God will defend the Right'. Providence Canning Town closed after being damaged (along with 60,000 other properties) in the Silvertown Explosion of 19 January 1917. A fire led to an explosion at a TNT plant; it was seen as far away as Maidstone.

Facing unrestricted u-boat warfare in the Atlantic in 1917 the government encouraged Sunday labour, supported by the Archbishop of Canterbury.[20] The AGM unanimously opposed this 'believing it to be contrary to the call of God and contrary to sound legislation'. At the AGM of March 1918, the scene was described as 'dark: war continued, sorrow was manifest on every hand, and the nation did not realise the need of Divine Guidance'. But by December the president celebrated mercy: 'what hath God wrought?' There was a cost. Looking back in 1941, S.G. Nunn noted 'our young men who served our country were either slain or came back from the war crushed and not able to render much help'.

The MASBC still stood strongly for truth. Liberalism was rife; evangelicals mounted an unsuccessful protest against the liberal president-elect, T.R. Glover, of the Baptist Union in 1923.[21] At the 1919 AGM the president, 'referring to the great efforts being made to unite all denominations said that he felt we had a strong call to come out and be separate from the confederacy'. The 1924 AGM expressed the 'gravest apprehension' about statements of the Free Church Federation at Brighton, affirming 'most emphatically our belief in the plenary and verbal inspiration of the Holy Scriptures; in the substitutionary character of the death of the Lord Jesus Christ; and we repudiate all effort that has in view union with the Romish Church'. To guard against downgrade, the MASBC added 'the plenary and verbal inspiration of the Old and New Testaments' to their doctrinal statement. Whilst many others fell away – the Brethren being a notable exception – the MASBC stood firm for truth.

Fifty years in, the MASBC had fallen from its 1901 peak but not everything was gloomy. From 1902 to 1922 whilst the number of churches fell from 66 to 50, the average membership rose slightly from 62 to 65 and the average Sunday school size was 150. In 1918 with membership, baptisms, teachers and scholars all down, the urge was to 'strengthen the things that remain' including the 'Christian duty' of 'welcoming strangers into our churches'. A 1922 proposal to extend the Association's area was dropped after criticism from the Charity Commissioners. The Association had reasonably healthy finances with £9,482 in stocks (£275,000 today) plus around half that loaned to churches. There were also an increasing number of pastors: 60% of churches were pastorless in 1902 but by 1926 this was down to 35%. There was a base from which to build.

Phase II: Increasing evangelistic urgency (1921–71)
Spreading the faith (inter-war years)

The inter-war years saw vigorous evangelism from evangelical churches not infected by liberalism and the MASBC also began to display increasing evangelistic urgency. The 1925 half yearly meeting issued a positive call: 'that the Committee consider whether anything can be done to increase and extend evangelistic work in the Churches'. The committee ratified the executive's suggestions of a small hymnbook for open air meetings and mission services, the formation of a Home Mission section and a public meeting. The March 1926 AGM resolved to write to churches 'urging the importance of endeavouring to reach the people in their neighbourhood, and offering the assistance which the Committee can give in response to the expressed wish and application of each individual Church'. The committee failed to appoint a Home Evangelism sub-committee because no-one was prepared to be left out! A 1928 special meeting for pastors and deacons asked 'that the Committee consider the question as to how sites and buildings can be provided for Strict Baptist Churches in districts where such causes do not exist'.

Sunday schools mattered. In 1928 it was stated that

80% of members had passed through them. Retention was discussed in 1933 as part of 'ways and means of disseminating the Gospel'. Highbury ran an annual 'Old Scholars' Rally' for those who once attended Sunday school. In 1934 the Fellowship of Youth (FOY) was formed to 'stay the leakage of our young people when they leave the Sunday School'. Literature, rallies and summer camps followed. The FOY played a key part for many years to come. Evangelism went beyond youth. Home Mission found women's meetings and open air meetings encouraging at Bethnal Green in 1936.

Increasing evangelistic urgency was not universal. At a special committee in 1944 one man commented on the 'urgent need for an evangelical witness throughout the denomination'. W.S. Baker (at the end of a quarter of a century as general secretary) proposed a number of resolutions. It was agreed 'that we should be more fully engaged than we are in the working of preaching the Gospel to those that are without' and 'that a circular be sent to all our Churches pointing out the necessity of Evangelistic effort, and offering such help as may be needed'.

Seeking fellowship (inter-war years)

At MASBC meetings the 'Strict Baptist denomination' was often mentioned: all holding such doctrines. In 1930 the MASBC requested 'kindred Associations in this country, and also the Strict Baptist Churches in India, in Australia, Canada, and elsewhere be asked to unite with us in prayer during this week of prayer'. Delegates were sent to the AGMs of the Suffolk and Norfolk Association and the Cambridge Union and there was a regular exchange of preachers. The Strict Baptist Trust for funding pastors was set up encompassing the Cambridgeshire Union, Northern Union, Suffolk and Norfolk Association, Strict & Particular Baptist Society and Gospel Standard Societies. All churches in the London area (except Gospel Standard) were urged by letter to join in 1932. In the same year, an unusually evocative minute records that Ernest Kevan 'pleaded for a closer union with our friends in the North[ern Union]'. The president was positive on fellowship but not union. In 1933, Buckland Common near Tring wanted to join but was instead referred to the Northern Union!

Sharing funds (inter-war years)

The MASBC wanted to stay up to date. The secretary got

a telephone in 1928 and the Association had to trace out representatives of the last survivor of the original Loan Fund trustees when it realised that the Association was not the trustee! Discussing funding for a boiler issue at Eltham in 1936 'Mr Grimwood expressed the opinion that the time is long overdue for doing away with boilers, and that electric radiators were an unqualified success'. Bromley were therefore granted £10 towards the £91 cost of 'economical' electric heating. An interesting snapshot is provided in 1940 by the eight Chesham men standing as sureties for a £165 loan. Their jobs were: woodenware manufacturer, joiner, auxiliary policeman, insurance agent, decorator, civil servant, clerk and two decorators.

In 1932, Honorary General Secretary Pastor W.S. Baker learned that Little Wild Street Chapel had been sold. He argued that, since it had been a Strict and Particular Baptist church from 1691 to 1870 the Association ought to benefit, and negotiated to spend that money not just in the local parishes but right across 'the County of London'. MASBC received one-third of the funds - £11,871 (over £500,000 today). Initial applications were approved: a contribution towards a Chadwell Street deaconess over three years, Highbury manse, Lewisham freehold, Notting Hill Gate pastoral support, Courland Grove electric light, Wandsworth Sunday school and Home Mission, Greenwich organ and stairs to pulpit and Hornsey Rise loan repayment. In 1934 applications were limited to 'be an inducement to Churches to launch out on new ventures'. The fund is still helping London churches today.

Standing on fundamentals

The MASBC was happy to add to the doctrinal statement to refute error. In 1936 the deity of Christ was addressed. Some prominent Strict Baptists, like John Stevens, had denied eternal sonship. They held that references to Christ as Son referred to his human not divine nature, and references to the Son's existence before birth regarded his soul not his godhead. As late as 1926, *Gospel Standard* (GS) editor, J.K. Popham, contrasted the orthodoxy of GS churches to the error of Earthen Vessel churches on this doctrine.[22] In 1936 a notorious 1860 *Earthen Vessel* article was dredged up where eternal sonship was dubbed 'a piece of twaddle' and 'a metaphysical conceit'.[23] This stung because the *The Earthen Vessel and Gospel Herald* was now the official MASBC publication.

The original doctrinal basis had skirted the controversy: the word 'Son' does not appear in any clause! The Trinitarian clause was vague: 'the equality and distinct personality of the Father, the Word, and the Holy Ghost in the unity of the Godhead'. The 1936 AGM strongly affirmed Trinitarian orthodoxy. It strengthened the first clause of the doctrinal basis by substituting 'Son' for 'Word' and stating that Father, Son and Holy Ghost 'are equal in eternity, substance, power and glory'. It then added a substantial second clause ruling out any vestige of error: 'in the fullness of time God sent forth His Son, ever subsisting in Essential Deity, who was conceived by the Holy Ghost, and born of the Virgin Mary, so that our Lord Jesus Christ is very God and very Man in one complex person'. In 1965 a further Christological statement was added: 'the personal and bodily return of our Lord Jesus Christ'.

The MASBC wanted truth lived out. In 1926, losing children from Sunday school was largely attributed to 'parents who go motoring on Sundays and take their children with them'. In 1931 they urged the Home Secretary against any opening of Sunday cinemas or places of entertainment. The letter summoning delegates to 1930's AGM lamented the 'abounding error of our times'. In 1938 the committee telegraphed Salem Brighton (Bond Street) to prohibit appointment of a pastor who was out of step with its trust deed. In 1938 Ernest Kevan publicly 'urged the need for the preparation of cheap readable literature setting forth the doctrines of the denomination'. Truth was to be confessed, taught and applied.

The stand for truth continued post-war. In 1949 the president announced that it 'behoved us who hold the doctrines of God's Word and grace and the right order of Church fellowship not to admit of any compromise whatsoever'. Later examples of this are found in 1956 where there were both Itinerant Preachers' Exams and a letter to the MCC and seventeen counties protesting Sunday cricket. Although happy for the way ITV televised a service at Mt Zion, St John's Wood in 1965, the MASBC protested against other TV content. In 1961 Pastor Hogg urged the committee to write against 'the increase in sex and violence being broadcast ... at peak hours.' A special meeting in 1963 issued a telegram of protest against 'A Man Dies', a Christian rock opera on TV 'depicting the Crucifixion in a most blasphemous manner'.

Second World War

The Second World War was seen initially in spiritual terms. In 1936, President W.S. Baker noted 'forces are at work in the world, which were beyond the control of Statesmen'. In October 1938 there was a special day of prayer: 'in the interests of the low spiritual condition of many Strict Baptist Churches and the solemn events taking place on the Continent'. In 1939 Kevan stated: 'this was a time of crisis spiritually in which the quality of our faith and service would be tested'.

Soon the physical effects were felt. Paper rationing reduced the handbook size. Evacuation almost closed the Sunday schools. The blackout cancelled services and restricted evangelism – although pastors and members were witnessing in air-raid shelters. The blitz in 1940 saw nine churches damaged, MASBC men losing property and two involved in its churches killed. In his 1941 Presidential Address, S.G. Nunn, drew attention to the rarity of a non-pastor holding the office: he was a treasurer and Sunday school man. Nunn stated that 'much of this address has been penned amidst the sound of the buzz of aeroplanes, anti-aircraft gunfire, and even the dropping of bombs'. In 1943, the son of committee member W.M. Boorne was killed on active service. Despite bemoaning the hinderance of blackout restrictions to the end of the war, it was noted in 1944 that 'in saving us from further concentrated "fly-bomb" attacks the Lord has done great things for us'. As late as January 1945 the chapel at Chatham Road was destroyed by enemy action.

Female delegates at AGMs herald from the Second World War. In 1941 there was a female apology for absence. At the 1944 AGM 'the President gave a very warm welcome ... especially to Lady friends, several of whom were acting as delegates'. This led to a resolution to remove 'brethren' from Rule 4 to allow men or women to be delegates. Despite some contending that the MASBC should follow Scripture not expediency, the proposal carried 39-8.

Spreading the faith (post-war)

Post-war evangelism surged amongst evangelicals – the MASBC included. From 1948 there were week-long evangelistic campaigns with costs shared between church and Association. In 1949 Wandsworth placed a large poster at the railway station and reported: 'strangers had been brought in and there had been conversions'. There was a Hyde Park outreach at the end of May for several years and a rally at Bethesda, Notting Hill Gate in 1950 with the president speaking. The AGM unanimously endorsed a Home Mission proposal to appoint part-time or whole-time 'ministers-in-charge' for churches 'agreeable to accept such assistance.'

By 1945 the committee was seeking a voice in decisions regarding places of worship in the new housing estates. In 1952 MASBC's area was extended from 25 to 30 miles from St Paul's to accommodate one of sixteen sites for churches in Basildon (est. population 83,000). (This also allowed churches to join from Chelmsford, Stevenage, Luton, High Wycombe, Maidenhead and Guildford.) A decade later it broadened further to take in Essex, Hertfordshire, Middlesex, Buckinghamshire, Oxfordshire, Berkshire, Hampshire, Surrey, Sussex and Kent.

The decision to form a Basildon church led to 'a season of earnest supplication' by 'upwards of 15' committee members. C.B. Phillimore sold his business and left the church in Downe to plant. After visiting all 500 first homes, Phillimore reported he 'had yet to find a real Christian'. Phillimore also reported in 1953 'a large number of dedications of infants .... had given him an opportunity for having heart to heart talks with the parents'. Coaches from E & SE districts brought in believers for the stone laying. The outreach energised the MASBC, with the president stating in 1954 that 'it opened up a new vista for us as a people'. By September 1955 (just over two-and-half years in) there were forty-three members, three deacons and a Sunday school of 350. By February 1956, the membership stood at sixty-one and the church was approaching being self-sufficient (apart from the repayment of loans).

In 1956 the Association committed to the next plant: Gadebridge. Bexleyheath had surplus money after moving, so offered a £10,000 loan (£240,000 in today's money) to be 'invested for the benefit of the Church at Bexleyheath until required'. George Pibworth (president from 1956-7) became the church planter. In 1958 he was president of the local Free Church Council. The building opened in 1961 and there were regular appeals for workers as it was easier to get children to Sunday school (average attendance of 180 in 1962) than find people to teach them. By 1963 Gadebridge was just meeting its expenses but there was an appeal to other churches to repay the loan (10 shillings or more per member) so the loan fund could be used by other churches. The committee was not afraid to ask for money. In 1946, confronted with nineteen pastorless churches, forteen with part-time pastors and fifteen with whole-time pastors, 'the general feeling of the Committee was that Church members should be educated to realize the importance of giving as an act of worship'.

Seeking fellowship: National Union

The Second World War birthed an era of co-operation. Politically there was the United Nations. The International Council of Churches embraced a general Christian identity, John Stott advocated an Anglican identity and Lloyd-Jones stressed an evangelical identity. In this climate some MASBC men pursued the widest Strict Baptist unity possible.

In September 1942 a National Strict Baptist Union around the doctrinal basis of the Strict Baptist Trust & Pension Fund was proposed. 1945 saw a Joint-Conference of Strict Baptist Organisations in London 'to explore the possibility of a National Union'. A circular letter with a brochure for a National Federation was sent to 470 churches. In 1946 MASBC were encouraged by the 'warmth of feeling ... particularly from Non-associated churches'. However, fewer than a quarter of the churches joined this.

There was renewed impetus in 1962 with a 'Denominational Prayer Conference' at the Calvinistic Theological College where the MASBC representatives met with others from the Strict Baptist Mission, Suffolk and Norfolk Association, Cambridge and East Midlands Union, Strict and Particular Baptist Trust Corporation, Fellowship of Youth and National Federation. Another conference followed in 1963, opened and closed by Pastor Phillimore. The first prayer session's theme was 'a sincere appraisal of our past mistakes as responsible stewards in the household of our Lord and master'. There was agreement to work through differences and prepare a doctrinal basis for all the Strict Baptist Denomination.

In August 1965, E.J. Wood, president (1946-47) and pastor at Belvedere and Bexleyeath until his death in 1980, described the denominational Leicester conference as 'a moving and unforgettable experience of the Lord's presence'. For those seeking that 'ways and means of spreading among the churches the experience of the nearness of God' a series of prayer meetings were set up by the general secretary. At the 1966 AGM a proposed £50,000 appeal was set aside due to 'the deep need for a fresh outpouring of the Holy Spirit's power' coming above material or financial needs. In November Jack Hoad was proposing 'closer relationship with evangelical churches accepting the 1966 Affirmation of Faith'. In 1970 *The Gospel Herald* ceased in favour of *Grace Magazine*: a broader voice was more important than the MASBC voice. In the 1965-66 handbook, C.B. Phillimore rejoiced that a week's convention led by the second-blessing Arminian, Roy Hession, had 'provided a time of challenge and deepening of spiritual life'. The MASBC outlook had clearly broadened.

Phase III: Making of the modern Association (1971-2021)

Seeking fellowship: BEC

After the First World War, the MASBC looked increasingly outwards to the lost; after the 1960s it also looked increasingly outwards to other Christians. The 1960s were the turning point. Representatives attended the British Evangelical Council (BEC) conference in 1953, the year after it was founded by men like E.J. Poole-Connor. However, in 1954 the committee deemed it 'not sufficiently settled for the Denomination to be committed to joining at present'. In November 1964, the committee 'were in general sympathy with the aims of the [Evangelical Alliance] Conference' but left attendance 'to the liberty of churches'.

Evangelicals leaving mixed denominations encouraged a broader outlook. An observer was sent to the seminal National Association of Evangelicals in 1966 to hear Lloyd-Jones state: 'ecumenical people put fellowship before doctrine. We are evangelicals; we put doctrine before fellowship (Acts 2:42).'[24] The MASBC president, aware of imminent 'secession from the Baptist and Congregational Unions' stated that 'ministers and/or churches would be looking for spiritual fellowship and practical help. They might well turn to our denomination for support and assistance because of our uncompromising adherence to truth in the face of ecumenical pressures. We must be spiritually prepared to receive them.' In 1966 the committee decided by large majority to send a letter to Billy Graham assuring him of their prayers for his London crusade and to include nothing of their reservations regarding his 'co-operation with modernists'. They had already sent their handbook. Such an outlook was very different to twenty years before.

Lloyd-Jones' backing seems to have decisively changed the MASBC attitude to the BEC. At the 1968

AGM a decisive majority favoured joining, but the 75% threshold was only achieved in 1970 (allowing individual churches to opt out). In 1968, Jack Hoad's striking statement was carried without dissent, welcoming into fellowship 'all likeminded churches who affirm' or 'are not in any sense firmly opposed to' the 1966 Affirmation. In 1973 the MASBC paid £500 (today £4,000) towards a house for the BEC secretary.

The MASBC abstained on BEC membership for the Apostolic Church in 1977 but did not withdraw. During Robert Sheehan's presidency (1978-9) the secretary wrote a letter of protest when, in the first edition of *Foundations*, they felt that Paul Cook implied they were guilty of the 'sin of schism'. Shortly after leaving his Bexleyheath pastorate, Sheehan's book *Spurgeon and the Modern Church* articulated a separatist stance, certainly held by the MASBC in years past. But in 1985 the AGM, though divided, took a majority view to support the committee disassociating MASBC from the stance on the grounds it offended friends in the BEC. A glance at committee suggestions for AGM speakers from the 1980s onwards demonstrates the growing breadth of association.

Sharing funds: paid general secretary

A full-time general secretary was long in coming. When Pastor W.S. Baker retired in 1946 after over twenty-five years as honorary general secretary, the HYM heard of his 'worthy record of service unparalleled in the history of the Association'. He had seen the MASBC through incorporation and more. A special committee meeting proposed a full-time general secretary evangelist with a list of 'exacting qualifications' for 'a Christian statesmen of high grade'. Along with being a man of conviction with a sense of calling, the man was to be 'a well known denominational figure, highly respected for his gracious character and ability' and 'a first class preacher and an able administrator'. However, the matter was 'waived indefinitely' at the HYM. It resurfaced in 1970 with Jack Hoad becoming general secretary (part-time). He was asked to serve full-time in 1972, the appointment being ratified at both HYM and AGM in 1973. Four years on, an assistant to the secretary was appointed as a 'Minister of Religion with pastoral and administrative duties'.

Streamlining the structures

Following the extension of the Association's area in 1962, six suggestions were made for a change of name. The first listed was 'The Association of the Home & South Eastern Counties Strict Baptist Churches'. No decision was made. It was not until 1985 that a vote on 'The Association of Grace Baptist Churches South East' was taken. It just failed to make 75% but was ratified without debate the following year. The MASBC had become the AGBC(SE).

The restructuring of the Association was gradual but significant. For years the MASBC was led by a president, elected by the AGM for a year as vice-president, followed by a year as president. The president was invariably a minister who preached at meetings of sister associations and rallies. Presidents were men like E.J. Wood, Phillimore, Pibworth, Kevan, W.S. Baker and Sheehan. This was good for accountability, collegiality and variety. But it was less good for continuity and harder for a more geographically spread association. From 1951 the retiring president was allowed to remain on committee for a further year. In 1965 the need for quorums was ended and the maximum committee size doubled to fifty. The executive requested three years on committee before VP nomination in 1967 and two years were required by standing order in 1978. This reduced the options for VP. The final president was Gordon

Hoppe in 1985. A chairman followed, who was elected by the committee (not the AGM), who served three year terms. In 1988 an element of the previous system – a deputy chair – was rejected as binding someone in for six years. In 1993 the committee was reduced to twenty, not more than half pastors, along with the treasurer, general secretary, his assistant and the company secretary.

Increasingly power went to the executive. In 1970 the committee argued they had no position on effusion because the company were the trustees. In 1974 the executive of the committee became Executive Directors of Company. The main committee's meetings reduced from six to four a year and its business seemed to decrease. Coupled with the recent appointment of a full-time general secretary, this represented a significant change to the running of the Association. A company secretary was added to the executive in 1980. In the late 80s a committee member resigned, mentioning it seemed merely 'a "rubber stamp" for the executive'. The response was significant: 'Company business was reported on only for information, and that it was the province of the Directors to conduct the business of the Company.' Around the turn of the century a digest of committee minutes was sent out (with sensitive matters removed) to increase connection with the churches. Governance issues were unrecognisable from the early years of the Association. The need for legal and charity compliance and various policies had mushroomed, along with skill in managing various trust funds.

Meetings of the general and main committees decreased from the 1960s. With ongoing attendance challenges, the AGM and HYM could be on Saturdays from 1956. In 1973 the AGM was swapped to October and in 1980 the HYM dropped altogether amongst a swathe of changes. These included each church having four delegates at the AGM irrespective of church size and committee members needing one-third of the ballot (presumably to avoid them being automatically elected unopposed).

The place of women on the committee was debated. In 1974, with women joining the committee as district secretaries, a sub-committee was set up. It recommended that nominations for this position should be 'male members of MASBC churches of some years standing, having some knowledge of the other churches and their own church's recommendation, and be able to present our doctrinal position'. A 1988 study on the role of women failed to be published when the chairman said a 'majority vote' (11-8 with 3 abstentions) was not 'decisive in the circumstances'.

Standing on fundamentals: doctrinal basis

Duty faith

A decisive break from the past came in dropping the 'Duty Faith' clause. This followed the move of the Strict and Particular Baptist Society on its 1958 incorporation.[25] After an Eastbourne pastor's conference in 1977, Jack Hoad's 'Hypercalvinistic Distinctives and their relevance today' was circulated. The clause was dropped at the 1979 AGM. When one church advocated its reinsertion in 1985 and 1987 not a single church would second the motion.

Lord's Table

The Association's central distinguishing characteristic, its Lord's Table policy, was more nettlesome. There had always been some differences. In deciding not to comment on transient communion in 1944, the committee noted that the constitution was deliberately framed 'to include all Strict Baptists who are one in doctrine though not identical in practice'. By the 1980s people were moving around much more and MASBC churches were increasingly welcoming to those from other backgrounds. Often the table policy proved the main stumbling point. Increasingly Association churches wanted to show some pastoral flexibility whilst still making clear that the biblical order was for people first to believe, then to be biblically baptised and thus added to the church.

At the 1987 AGM the secretary, noting a legal opinion that trust deeds must be followed, suggested 'it would be unlikely that a judge would evict the church for failure to observe every letter of the law'. In 1991 one church wanted to welcome members in good standing from other churches (including paedobaptists) and was promised a meeting of three associations. In 1996 a statement both affirmed 'restricted communion' and the independence of local churches in its practical outworking, aiming for the 'best welfare of people rather than the maintenance of a set of rules'.

Explicit broadening came in 2014 with a carefully crafted new doctrinal statement. The old statement ruled out any paedobaptist receiving communion: 'the necessity of baptism by immersion ... in order to have

... admission to the Lord's Table'. In an 1871 context the deliberate ambiguity was on the type of Baptists welcomed, not stating whether these must be 'from the same faith and order' or just 'walking in the fear of God'. The 2014 chairman made clear the historic continuity, the AGM noting that the new 'Clause 10 is intended to uphold baptistic church order and a disciplined Lord's Table and a church could not in integrity subscribe to the Statement of Faith while permitting an open table in practice.' In the 2014 context (a fraction of the Christians of 1871) the deliberate ambiguity was on transient communion by stating that the Lord's Supper 'is administered under the discipline and pastoral care of the local church'. Unity was preserved and trust deed issues avoided by a judicious modernising of the wording. The new doctrinal basis, in line with other Grace Baptist organisations like GBM, also demonstrated how emphases had changed. Concerning sanctification, the first doctrinal basis highlighted the imperative: 'the absolute necessity for a holy life'. The 2014 version speaks of the means: that the Holy Spirit 'produces increasing likeness to Christ'.

Sharing the faith

The last fifty years of the Association saw a stabilisation in numbers. Despite the church planting endeavours in Basildon and Hemel Hempstead, the drop in numbers from 1922 to 1971 was huge. Although MASBC churches rose from 50 to 61, the average membership fell by over half from 65 to 32 whilst the average Sunday school attendance dropped by over two-thirds from 150 to 44. Conversely, the numbers from 1971 to 2021 were remarkably stable, with total membership just under 2,000 in 1971 and just over it in 2021. The number of churches is similar to the peak year (1901) but they are on average under half the size. Sunday school numbers are no longer collected.

Longstanding Association pastor and former general secretary, David Chapman, noted four factors which strengthened the Association during this period. First, there were more trained ministers. Before the 1960s theological training was the exception, but as this became increasingly common the churches gained a greater sense of direction. Second, BEC involvement meant MASBC churches were increasingly seen as an option for people relocating. The BEC/Affinity has been chaired by several Association general secretaries. Third, there was real evangelistic interest. A 1996 'Word in the World' residential conference drew in 120 to High Leigh, drawing in pastors beyond the Association. The Islington Gospel Outreach saw Highbury re-established. Hayes Lane set aside Tim Gardner as an evangelist. Nigel Hoad was appointed as the first director of Home Mission and involved in church planting in Ebbsfleet. Grace Baptist Partnership's work was positive in reviving struggling causes, often with radically different demographics to when they began, such as at Thamesmead. Fourth, there was a real emphasis on relationships between pastors. There was an away day for pastors and their wives. Work parties went to help other churches with one pastor of a small cause remarking that he had 'never felt more loved'.

The Association at 150

Over 150 years, the Association has become increasingly outward-looking. The MASBC began by Strict Baptists standing together, who then developed a greater urgency for evangelising together and eventually for connecting together with broader evangelicalism. The Association has always sought fellowship. It began within a more rigid Strict Baptist denomination and moved to broader Grace Baptist circles and Affinity.

The Association has always shared funds which have increased through shrewd stewardship. The Association has always stood firm for fundamental gospel truths. However, the number of its distinctives, its eagerness to contend for these and the homogeneity of church practice have all decreased over time. The Association has always been interested in sharing the faith. Initially this was establishing 'Strict Baptist causes' before the more evangelistic Home Mission developed over time.

Whilst the numerical highpoint was 1901, the climax of collaborative endeavour was probably the 1950s. A historian noted that 'not since the late Victorian period had there been such powerful evidence of a professing Christian people in Britain'.[26] The MASBC prayed for and experienced the Spirit's power in its church planting. The key turning point in the nature of the Association was the 1960s. It broadened in area, in collaboration with other Strict Baptists and in partnership with evangelicals. It led to the modern Association which is much less homogenous and whose distinctives (theological and practical) are less sharply defined. The 2021 AGBC(SE) is an association of calvinistic Baptist churches with a disciplined Lord's Table. Its fundamentals are positively set out in *Pure Church* (released by Grace Publications

Trust in 2018). Its members seek fellowship together as they share historic funds enabling them to spread the faith. Its challenge is to maintain its evangelistic vision and outward perspective whilst encouraging church members to embrace its biblical distinctives.

Happily the gospel heart of the Association is unchanged. At the 1875 AGM, President Hazleton preached these words:

> We are living in extraordinary times, and we are told that it is necessary that the Gospel should be so preached as to keep it abreast of the times ... It is necessary that it should be correctly, and (if you please) eloquently preached; but let it be the Gospel, let it be the words of Jesus Christ, and let us always go forth under a consciousness of the fact that the word of Christ will always be in advance of the times ... Whatever social or intellectual changes may take place, mankind will always be fallen creatures ... the robe of Christ's righteousness will then be needed, and the fountain of his blood will then be required.

If the AGBC(SE) survives another 150 years it will be by faithfulness to this timeless gospel that brings men and women up to date with their situation.

Notes

1. Kenneth Dix, *Strict and Particular: English Strict and Particular Baptists in the Nineteenth Century* (Baptist Historical Society, 2001), p. 216.
2. Dix, *Strict and Particular*, p. 192.
3. Augustus H. Strong, *Systematic Theology: A Compendium and Commonplace* (American Baptist Pub Society, 1907), pp. 973–5.
4. Geoffrey R. Breed, 'The London Association of Strict Baptist Ministers and Churches', *Baptist Quarterly* 35.8 (January 1994), p. 379 <https://doi.org/10.1080/0005576X.1994.11751953>
5. Seymour J. Price, 'London Strict Baptist Association, 1846–1853', *Baptist Quarterly* 9.2 (January 1938), p. 110 <https://doi.org/10.1080/0005576X.1938.11750456>
6. Breed, 'The London Association of Strict Baptist Ministers and Churches', p. 389.
7. Breed, 'The London Association of Strict Baptist Ministers and Churches', p. 391.
8. Cited in Robert Oliver, *History of the English Calvinistic Baptists: From John Gill to C.H. Spurgeon* (Edinburgh: The Banner of Truth Trust, 2006), p. 350.
9. William Jeyes Styles, *A Guide to Church Fellowship: As Maintained by Primitive Or Strict and Particular Baptists* (London, 1902), p. 77.
10. Styles, *A Guide to Church Fellowship*, pp. 78–9.
11. Dix, *Strict and Particular*, p. 277.
12. Cited in Dix, *Strict and Particular*, p. 201.
13. Dix, *Strict and Particular*, p. 204.
14. Dix, *Strict and Particular*, p. 207.
15. <https://www.open.ac.uk/Arts/building-on-history-project/resource-guide/source-guides/1851censusreport.pdf> (accessed 31 May 2021).
16. Richard Mudie-Smith, *The Religious Life of London* (Hodder &

Stoughton, 1904), p. 448.
17. Dix, *Strict and Particular*, p. 162.
18. <www.visionofbritain.org.uk/data_cube_page.jsp?data_theme=T_POP&data_cube=N_TOT_POP&u_id=10097836&c_id=10001043&add=N> (accessed 8 April 2021).
19. Dix, *Strict and Particular*, p. 197.
20. <https://hansard.parliament.uk/Commons/1917-03-15/debates/1adf3cb5-8f25-43a2-85ba-706c81356932/SundayLabourOnLand> (accessed 17 August 2021).
21. David W. Bebbington and David Ceri Jones, *Evangelicalism and Fundamentalism in the United Kingdom During the Twentieth Century* (Oxford University Press, 2013), p. 106.
22. Barrington Raymond White, *Pilgrim Pathways: Essays in Baptist History in Honour of B.R. White* (Mercer University Press, 1999), p. 20.
23. White, *Pilgrim Pathways*, p. 19.
24. Iain H. Murray, *Evangelicalism Divided: A Record of Crucial Change in the Years 1950 to 2000* (Banner of Truth Trust, 2000), p. 46.
25. P. Toon, 'English Strict Baptists', *Baptist Quarterly* 21.1 (January 1965), p. 33 <https://doi.org/10.1080/0005576X.1965.11751170>
26. Callum G. Brown, *The Death of Christian Britain: Understanding Secularisation 1800-2000* (Routledge, 2009), p. 5.

4

UK Mission and Church Planting

Nigel Hoad & Barry King

'In all my prayers for all of you, I always pray with joy because of your partnership in the gospel from the first day until now ...' (Phil. 1:4–5).

In this chapter, we will consider the potential of co-operative, associational efforts for facilitating local mission and church planting in the United Kingdom. We will do so anecdotally by looking at what the Association of Grace Baptist Churches (South East) – from here simply referred to as the 'Association' – together with Grace Baptist Partnership have achieved in recent years with the Lord's help, as well as some of the challenges that have been faced and overcome. The key lesson is that although it has been far from easy, more can be done together.

For many years, the Association has been involved in gospel partnership, that is, working alongside other churches, whether that be with plants, replants, or established congregations. This is at the heart of the Association's mission. Such co-operation has involved everything from working as teams through to the use of a single evangelist. It has been encouraging to recently see, for example, the gospel partnership occurring in Grace Church Brighton, where local evangelical churches, individuals connected with the Sussex Gospel Partnership, Grace Church Guildford, Cuckfield Baptist Church, and Grace Baptist Trust Corporation have worked together.

In the same way, although with far less central involvement, it has been good to see local churches getting together to plant new churches, and the latest at Didcot is a fine example. There, the co-operation between the churches in Abingdon and Hanney with Jim and Helen Sayers, along with additional support from Grace Baptist Mission and the Association, demonstrate what can be achieved. Local Christians, many of whom are members of Abingdon and Hanney, formed a core team and over the next few months (from the time of writing), will constitute as a local church.

We could turn the clock back several years, and note the gospel partnership through the London Inreach Project in Soho, which in later years saw the Association get more involved, from giving property advice, to engineering the acquisition, refurbishment, and management of a local butcher's shop into a state of the art Fairtrade shop. Believers from a range of other churches who helped run the shop through the week made this a happy and productive partnership, building on the legacy of Michael and Pam Toogood, Mike and Gwen Mellor, Derek and Rachel Sewell, and finally, but still over many years, Andrew and Joy Murray. The shop project could never have got off the ground without gospel partnership, and the friendships that were spawned as a result have outlasted the shop, which sadly (but probably beneficially) had to close due to the redevelopment of Berwick Street. Currently the Association is helping the work in Covent Garden through Tim Gardner, who is seconded by Hayes Lane Baptist Church to work with Home Mission, another aspect of associational co-operation. Indeed, Tim, together with Maria Amoako-Britten from Highbury Baptist Church, have worked and continue to work alongside several of our Association churches.

The Islington Gospel Outreach team is in the same era as the Soho church plant. Under the leadership of Geoff Gobbett, the team helped re-establish Highbury Baptist Church. Other members of that team have gone on to serve churches throughout the Association, and now further afield, even overseas. Partnership is like a stone causing ever-widening ripples in God's kingdom pond.

We can write of the partnership of Grace Baptist Trust Corporation, Grace Baptist Partnership, and the Association in replanting of a church in Halstead, Essex, where Graham Field is now the pastor. We can mention the replanting of the work at Chingford, north-east London, where the support of Grace Baptist Partnership alongside the existing church and Association over the last ten years has, humanly speaking, been critical to the work continuing to this day. Here, the co-operation between the local church and the Association began when the then church pastor and sole deacon approached the Association to ask whether they would look at replanting the church, as they were both standing down and leaving the church in a vulnerable position. After a period of prayerful examination, the Association believed it was right to help, and in God's goodness, the church continues its witness today. With regard to Chingford, gospel partnership has seen an Association church – Hayes Lane Baptist Church in Bromley – send one of its men, Bernard Roberts, together with his wife Michelle, to become the pastor. Recently a new pastor, Grayson Fuhrman, was introduced to the church through Grace Baptist Partnership's connections. The work has known the faithful support of Grace Baptist Church Wood Green, as well as the invaluable evangelistic support of Daniel Shwe from Grace Baptist Church North Watford, and the Grace Baptist Partnership. In a replant situation like Chingford, the Association has worked closely with the church, and Nigel Hoad (director of Home Mission), with the agreement of the church, and has acted as a quasi-elder alongside the pastor. This role has drawn the church and Association closer together, and we trust it has been of much benefit and encouragement to the church and pastor. In another demonstration of gospel partnership, the Particular Baptist Fund has supported the employment of the pastor and provided a loan to replace an old leaky roof. Partnership, as we have said before, takes many forms, but all with the common aim of seeing souls saved and churches strengthened, all to the praise of God's glory.

Associational co-operation with the church at Devonshire Drive, Greenwich, is not dissimilar to what has happened at Chingford, with the church asking the Association to oversee replanting a new church. Home Mission had worked with the church for some years in advance of this request, so its culture, context, community, and gospel opportunity was well known before the Association initiated the replant. Nigel Hoad again served as a quasi-elder and Tim Gardner helped with street evangelism with both the pioneer pastor and his successor, Rodrigo Rampazzo. It has been a privilege and joy to see a new church forming from local young professional families, and students from Greenwich University. In Greenwich, the now renamed Village Church has enjoyed a good relationship with Grace Church, an evangelical Anglican plant, with the added twist that one of its pastors was also a lecturer of Rodrigo when he attended Proclamation Trust's Cornhill Training Course. Gospel partnerships, as we have seen, can take various forms, and in Greenwich this has included renting out premises to Grace Church

Greenwich and a local Brazilian church. The Village Church's pastor, Rodrigo, is Brazillian and his wife, Jordan, is American, so it is no surprise that the church has a very cosmopolitan feel and as Greenwich is one of London's most popular tourist destinations, this has caused the church to enjoy a consistent footfall of visitors to its Sunday and midweek meetings.

Working together with Grace Baptist Partnership has also been evidenced in joint and parallel evangelism training initiatives. Training is an essential part of each organisation's ministry, picking up the scriptural exhortation to equip God's people for works of service. While, generally, that exhortation is meant for the local church context, most often the Association and Grace Baptist Partnership have partnered with local churches or groups of churches to provide this training, borne out of their shared experience, and personal application of the biblical principles and practices of evangelism. For the Association, there has been the added joy of serving among churches outside of its geographic area.

The story of Grace Baptist Partnership – a relatively new initiative amongst Grace Baptists in the United Kingdom – is inextricably tied to the Association. In early 2003, Barry King, joined by his family and a small group of others, began worshipping and witnessing in the London Borough of Haringey. They formed an independent evangelical church with the Second London Baptist Confession of Faith serving as their doctrinal basis. Meeting as an independent church in rented accommodation, they were unaware of the existence of the Association.

One day, as Barry and his family walked along Wood Green High Street, they encountered a man distributing tracts. The man, Ben Cunningham, was the pastor of the Grace Baptist church meeting on Park Ridings behind the shopping centre in Wood Green. He and Barry – both originally from the United States – chatted briefly and agreed to meet up at some stage to get better acquainted. Neither of them could have envisioned that their brief conversation would set in motion a chain of gospel events that continues to this day.

Not long after that first meeting, the church Barry was leading needed to find a place to baptise three new believers. Ben offered the use of the baptismal pool in the building at Park Ridings, and also asked Barry to think about something. He and his wife were considering a call to serve the Lord elsewhere in England. They felt it was right to accept the call but were concerned about what would happen with the work in Wood Green. The numbers were low and it was possible the church might even close.

Ben suggested that the church Barry was leading meet jointly with the church on Park Ridings for a period of three months of weekly worship and fellowship. The arrangement was agreed by both congregations and Barry and Ben shared the ministry for the next several months. It was during this time that the two congregations became one. Ben accepted the call to serve elsewhere and Barry was appointed pastor of the amalgamated church.

It was through this amalgamation in 2005 that Barry and others in the church came into fellowship with the Association. It was through this fellowship that they came to know men such as David Chapman, David Whitmarsh, Nigel Hoad, and Geoff Gobbett. It was through their relationships with these men that further church planting opportunities in Angel and North Watford came the way of the church in Wood Green. A genuine partnership in the gospel was developing even before Grace Baptist Partnership was officially formed.

To this point, all of the activities of the Wood Green

church had been in concert with the Association. However, as new opportunities further afield emerged, - such as in Halstead (Essex) and Edlesborough (Buckinghamshire) - this began to change. The previous church in Halstead was a member of another association. The previous church in Edlesborough was not a member of any association at all. This meant the work of what would become Grace Baptist Partnership was both within as well as outside the orbit of the Association.

As the work increasingly gathered momentum, the formation of Grace Baptist Partnership became a practical necessity. However, for the avoidance of doubt, the Partnership was never intended to be a competitor with the Association but rather a means through which the Association, other regional associations, and even Grace Baptist churches which were not in any association at all, might co-operate in church planting and revitalisation.

In keeping with this philosophy, Barry King - who served on the Association's main committee, executive committee, and Home Mission sub-committee - was selected to serve as the general secretary of the Partnership. David Chapman - at that time general secretary of the Association - was chosen as chairman of the Partnership. Even though Barry has since moved out of London and serves a church that is not a member of the Association and David has retired from his Association role, Philip Woodley serves as both a member of the Association main and executive committees as well as a trustee of the Partnership.

Though the work of the Partnership beyond the geographical boundaries of the Association was extending, its role within the Association was ongoing – and expanding. The Partnership and Association would work closely in the revitalisation of the church in Thamesmead, and the replanting of churches in Grays and Chingford. Additionally, as newly planted or replanted churches in Edlesborough, Southall, and Halling were formally constituted, they requested admission into Association membership. In more recent years, we have worked co-operatively in Hyde Heath, Walthamstow, and Bexleyheath as well.

Our mutual interest and involvement in Walthamstow and Bexleyheath were, in God's providence, in many ways a result of the church revitalisation work in Thamesmead. The story of how that work began gives a good insight into how the Association and the Grace Baptist Partnership worked together, particularly – but not exclusively – in those days.

In 2009, Barry King, then pastor of the church in Wood Green and member of the Association's Home Mission sub-committee, was asked by Nigel Hoad to visit Thamesmead and Greenwich. Nigel hoped that Barry might have some insights into how to help the church at Thamesmead which had gone a number of years without a pastor as well as how to prepare the church at Greenwich for the retirement of their pastor in the then foreseeable future. Barry, along with his sons Regan and Ryan – now both pastors of Association churches – spent a day exploring these two very different places in south-east London.

When the time came to report back to Nigel Hoad and David Chapman, Barry shared his deep concern for the work in Thamesmead. With so many positive things in place – a committed core of members, a number of non-members in regular attendance, active prayer support for the local district of churches, and a willingness to help from the wider Association – it seemed only right to seek to revitalise this church and thus enable them to more effectively evangelise their gospel-needy area. But who would be prepared to lead such an effort?

Nigel enquired as to whether or not Barry might

have the capacity alongside his other work to take an active role in moving the work in Thamesmead forward. Barry was willing, but needed some help getting his head around how it would work practically. Together they developed a locum pastor model which would be field tested at Thamesmead. Barry would preach each Sunday at Thamesmead for three months. He would continue to preach one Sunday a month for an additional nine months. He would lead a midweek Bible study and prayer meeting for the entire twelve months of the locum pastorate.

It looked very good on paper but would it work in practice? Additionally, would the church in Wood Green be willing to release him for this endeavour? And, most importantly, would the church at Thamesmead be willing to receive him? Nigel – with help from David Chapman – would take the lead in bringing the Thamesmead church on board. Barry would speak to the church in Wood Green to gain their support. By God's grace both churches agreed to the proposal and a start date of January 2010 was agreed.

On the first Saturday of January 2010, friends from the local district of Grace Baptist churches recruited by Nigel Hoad, converged on Thamesmead for a day of work and witness. The church building received a deep clean and the task of painting and decorating commenced. While a band of willing workers laboured away inside, others began the process of taming the garden, while still others distributed leaflets in the area inviting people to attend the Sunday services.

There was a real degree of expectancy as people gathered for the service the next morning. The sense that God was doing something was palpable. The weeks which followed – though not without their challenges – were filled with encouragements. As the people met week by week for worship and worked through *Nine Marks of a Healthy Church* with Barry at a midweek meeting, the core membership of the church was strengthened and others were added to their number.

Even as those leading the work rejoiced in what God was doing in the present, their concern for the future leadership of the church remained. Barry had been in discussions with Derek Sewell, then serving with the London Inreach Project, about the possibility of taking up the leadership of a church planting project in Suffolk. One night as they travelled back to London from Ipswich, Barry told Derek about what had been happening at Thamesmead. In the end, Derek would not go to Suffolk but would take up the pastorate of the Thamesmead church. He has now served faithfully – and fruitfully – in that role for more than a decade.

In one way, perhaps the most significant thing to come out of the Thamesmead project was the raising up of new leaders not only for that church but in time for other churches as well. Among those baptised during Barry's locum pastorate were Chola Mukanga and Wale Akinrogunde. As both of them matured in their personal discipleship and theological understanding, it became evident that the Lord was going to use them for his glory in the church at Thamesmead. Additionally, both men had a genuine burden for other churches, particularly other churches in their part of London. After the church at Bexleyheath lost their pastor, Barry spent a number of weeks preaching there and helping them think through their future. In time, both Chola and Wale would begin preaching at Bexleyheath on a supply basis. As Chola's conviction that he should lay aside secular employment and pursue full-time pastoral ministry grew, the church's appreciation of his ministry grew as well. In time they would appoint him to serve as their pastor, which he has done since late-2016. Chola's concern for other churches still remains as he has sought to encourage other churches in his locality. Additionally, he has served the churches more widely through Grace Baptist Partnership – first as a trustee, then as treasurer, and now as chairman.

God was also at work in Wale, who found many useful avenues for service in the Thamesmead church. In time, with the encouragement of Barry and the support of the church, he commenced studies at London Seminary. It was during his time of study that he was chosen to lead the church-replanting project at Walthamstow; he would complete his studies on a part-time basis while also serving as a church planter. The difficulties of balancing study and service were not enough to dent Wale's enthusiasm for serving the Lord. He would complete his course at London Seminary and the church in Walthamstow was recently constituted with Wale being appointed as pastor. The work jointly undertaken in Thamesmead has ultimately served not only to advance the gospel there, but in at least two other parts of London as well!

One of the larger church planting projects that gospel partnership was involved in was the Gateway Project in Ebbsfleet. Tasked in 2004 to explore the viability of a new church plant in the south east of England, the then

Government's plans to proceed with a massive housing programme along the Thames Estuary provided a ready-made opportunity. A steering group was set up with pastors from several Association churches, as well as from local FIEC and evangelical Anglican churches, all with experience and expertise. Six years of preparatory work confirmed the need and opportunity to church plant in this area of the south east, and a location within the new Garden City of Ebbsfleet, astride the Eurostar high speed train route, was selected. The aims and objectives of the church plant were agreed, and advertising was placed for a team leader in 2010.

The limited response to what was considered a 'golden opportunity' to serve the Lord was a blow, as was the decision, because of an economic down-turn, to delay the construction of the first housing in Ebbsfleet at Castle Hill. But the Lord had his man! Barry King, part of the steering group, had spoken with Adam and Julia Laughton, then pastoring Grace Baptist Church Southport. The Laughtons then, suitably encouraged, responded to the advert. Their view of the position, forever etched into the memory, was that the project was calling for 'Superman'. However, Adam in due course was invited and accepted the role of team leader, and with the encouragement of his home church, headed south with Julia and their family of four, to set up home in Gravesend in August 2011. In taking that decision, the Lord graciously affirmed the project, as it would have been easy for Adam and Julia to say 'yes, but ...' and remained in Southport. After all, at the time, Ebbsfleet didn't exist – apart from an international train station.

Associational partnership again played a significant role at this point. Church planting should, in most cases, be a local church initiative. Here it was centrally led by the Association, and yet the Lord graciously built a relationship with Hope Baptist Church in Gravesend, an Association church, just a few miles from where Ebbsfleet would be built. Their pastor, Stephen Lloyd, was on the steering group for the project, part of the interview panel, and party to the decision to invite Adam to the team leadership. It was also largely with Stephen's foresight that rather than delay the process because of the lack of houses, a start could be made to gain experience of a house church plant in an area of Gravesend not far from Ebbsfleet. Adam and Julia bought into this revised plan, and so a house was purchased, which became a family home and base for the church plant for the next nine years. Only this last year have Adam and Julia been able to move into Castle Hill, Ebbsfleet.

Paul tells the Ephesians that they (and we) 'are God's handiwork, created in Christ Jesus to do good works, which God prepared in advance for us to do' (Eph. 2:10). An early partnership was established with the then landowner and major developer, Land Securities. They proved to be supportive, understanding, and helpful – probably helped by the fact that they had been a client of Nigel Hoad's while he was employed in the construction industry and knew some of the people involved. This was one of several instances of God going ahead of the church plant. Another partnership that quickly developed and is still maintained was with the Baptist Union's church plant leader for Ebbsfleet, Penny Marsh. Penny is a godly, evangelistically passionate woman, who helped us to know more of the background to the development, key personalities, and early opportunities to get involved in the community, once construction was underway. We do not agree on everything, but another lesson learned in church planting in a new town is that most people couldn't care less about 'which church' – they were glad that residents, including Christians, were caring for them and representing them, and we could do that better together than separately.

With construction eventually well underway, the church plant could become actively involved in the emerging community and engaged in evangelism. Another wonderful partnership was the financial support of the Particular Baptist Fund for the project, a partnership which has only this year come to an end after ten years of financial support. Five years ago, and halfway through the initial ten-year plan, a major review of the project was carried out, with the biggest outcome being the move of Nigel and Lucy Hoad to live in Castle Hill. A couple had previously been sought, through various means, to live in Castle Hill – but to no avail. Perhaps church planting in a totally new town that is being built around you with virtually no community facilities, and no traditional church building (there are none and unless the Anglicans get their way, there will not be any traditional church or other faith buildings in Ebbsfleet), trumped the entrepreneurial risk of church planting with a blank sheet of paper? In any case, Nigel and Lucy moved into Castle Hill in December 2016, and the project took on a more localised and focussed lead. Largely built on personal relationship and community involvement, church planting in Ebbsfleet has been slow and hard work. Relationships have been built, community involvement has taken place, Christmas and Easter outreach activities have been enjoyed by the residents, but to date there have been no known conversions. Yet, the project was born with the purpose to grow a new church through conversion! What has the Lord been doing?

Difficulties and discouragements aside, God's partnership with the church plant has established a new church. Grace Church Ebbsfleet was constituted in February 2018 and in 2021 became an independent church, employing Adam as her pastor. The church has twelve members, and several residents have joined the Sunday afternoon Connect meetings and Wednesday afternoon Craft Club. House Church is still a hard concept for outsiders, and even Christians. It has its advantages and its disadvantages, not least in 2020-21, during the Covid-19 restrictions. But all in all, the house church model has provided a real family base in the heart of the community that people may struggle to enter for a 'service' but are very willing to enjoy in hospitality, a cry for help, and a common cause to see the new development become a good place to live for everyone. Partnership was key to the concept of

Ebbsfleet, and still is the heartbeat of the church plant, from the members to its supporters and the churches.

In serving the Lord alongside one another for more than a decade, leaders of the Association of Grace Baptist Churches (South East) and the Grace Baptist Partnership have learned many valuable lessons. A few of these are outlined below.

Relationships

Perhaps the most vital lesson any of us has learned is the importance of relationships. Our work together has not been organisational in nature so much so as it has been relational. From the beginning, the principal players genuinely liked one another. No, we didn't spend a lot of time together socially but through phone calls, email correspondence, and regular meetings we were in frequent contact with one another. When David Chapman retired from his service as Association secretary and Barry relocated outside of London to lead a church replanting work in Edlesborough alongside his wider work with Grace Baptist Partnership, regular opportunities for meeting up for discussion and fellowship were not as easy to come by. Adequate time was not invested – for various reasons – in cultivating new relationships and deepening existing ones. We are grateful that in the past year much relational strength has been restored and we are looking forward to serving the Lord alongside one another in mutually beneficial ways in the coming years.

Spiritual maturity

We have, likewise, often been reminded of the importance of spiritual maturity in our relationships and joint service. Whenever we have been willing to defer to one another, to give one another the benefit of the doubt, and to always speak well of one another, our partnership has flourished. When personal insecurity and professional jealousy has crept in, our fellowship – and partnership – has been weakened. Again, we rejoice in the sanctifying work of the Spirit in each other's lives and can testify to the fact that prospects for ongoing partnership are bright.

Kingdom-minded

We have all had to learn not to be territorial. This is not the Association's work. This is not the Partnership's work. This is not even our personal work. This is the Lord's work. This has been a useful reminder when the role one group has played in a project has been applauded while the role another group has played has been overlooked. None of us have sought our own glory or to enhance the reputation of our own organisation. It is regrettable though that at times others have sought to pit us against one another. We've never, by God's grace, been *for* much less *against* one another. We have been for the fulfilment of God's purposes among the churches – nothing more, nothing less.

Distinct

We have also needed to learn to work together without becoming one another. Both the Association and the Partnership have their unique strengths as well as their inherent weaknesses. Working in close co-operation promotes mutuality, which is good. But one of the most beneficial aspects of partnership is the catalytic effect the individuality of each partner has on the other. We've not always got this right, but when we have our partnership has been at its best.

We live in a day of unprecedented opportunity for the gospel. We know of dozens of churches that need to be revitalised; hundreds of places where new churches need to be planted, and untold thousands – indeed, millions – who remain without God and without hope in the world. There are challenges associated with partnering together on any level. However, partnership for the sake of the gospel is a biblical as well as practical necessity. The Association of Grace Baptist Churches (South East) and Grace Baptist Partnership have sought this kind of biblical partnership in previous years and will, by God's grace, continue to do so in years to come.

5

Overseas Associations: Peru and Italy

Leonardo De Chirico & Jaime D. Caballero

Wherever Baptist churches exist, the issue of forming associations of churches is relevant. This chapter shall deal with some specific opportunities and challenges for associations of churches in two overseas contexts: Peru and Italy. By way of making reference to specific stories and backgrounds in Latin American and European contexts, it will also draw some more general lessons that readers from other places could hopefully benefit from.

Why Peru and Italy? Because the authors come from there: Jaime Daniel Caballero from Peru and Leonardo

De Chirico from Italy, respectively. In both countries and more broadly across Latin America and Europe, the evangelical witness – including that of Baptist churches – has taken place in a context profoundly shaped by Roman Catholicism. Roman Catholicism's influence is especially visible in areas of doctrine, devotion, and culture. Many evangelical converts are from Roman Catholic backgrounds, and churches inevitably face the challenge in congregational life of confrontation with a distinctly Roman Catholic way of doing things, from which they want to distance themselves.

Of course, Peru and Italy sharply differ on many other accounts. In Peru, as across Latin America, evangelical churches have significantly grown over the last few decades while in Italy the gospel witness struggles to move beyond a very limited impact. Peru is also culturally different from the European milieu of Italian life. This being the case, the chapter's two authors will address the same issues separately, so as to give a contextualised answer. Their unique contributions will be preceded by the initials JDC (Jaime Daniel Caballero) and LDC (Leonardo De Chirico).

Why are associations of churches necessary?

JDC: There are two things that almost all Latin American countries have in common: colonialism and Roman Catholicism. These have affected Latin American churches in two different ways.

First, Roman Catholicism provided the basic structure upon which Protestantism developed. For most Latin American countries, Roman Catholicism is still the official religion. Open and public evangelisation and the establishment of new churches among the native population was forbidden in Peru until 1962, when it became permitted with the end of the Second Vatican Council (1959-62). The vast majority of missionaries began to arrive after this date – primarily from North America and evangelical churches saw exponential growth during the 1980s and 1990s. At best then, we are dealing with a very young evangelical church, with relatively little time having passed since its founding.

Second, colonialism had a double effect. On the one hand, it generated financial and intellectual dependence on both the United States and Europe. On the other hand, it created unnecessary and often non-existent divisions within the continent, which made it difficult to unite churches with a common background and history, who were nonetheless politically in two different countries.[1]

With these considerations in mind I would like to give five reasons why associations of churches are indispensable in Peru, and more broadly, Latin America.

Firstly, although the Latin American evangelical church is very large numerically, it is weak in economic and theological resources. The vast majority of Protestant churches are located in the poorest economic sectors of society, in contrast to the Roman Catholic church. This makes it difficult to establish seminaries, plant churches, and send out missionaries on an independent basis. From a theological perspective, the vast majority of pastors have little or no formal theological training. The only way this can be resolved is through the united efforts of several churches.

Secondly, there is an inability to care for the physical needs of pastors. Since the evangelical church is not officially recognised by the state in the same way that the Roman Catholic church is, most pastors do not have life insurance, access to a retirement pension, or state medical care. In fact, they are not listed as workers, and are excluded from almost all state benefits and legal protection. One of the central purposes of an association of churches in this context would be the legal protection and care that pastors could not otherwise have.

Thirdly, developing contextualised church models. Several of the church planting models used in Latin America have proven to be inefficient at best. A well-known model used in the US is the 1% rule, proposed by Lyle Schaller, and popularised by Timothy Keller.[2] The model proposes the following:

> Every year, any association of churches should plant new congregations at the rate of 1 percent of its existing total; otherwise, that association is in maintenance and decline. If an association wants to grow more than 50 percent [in a generation], it should plant 2 to 3 percent per year.[3]

The viability of such a church planting model presupposes a tremendous readiness of human and financial resources. The reality of Lima or Medellín is different from that of New York or San Francisco. Unless strong church associations are formed in Latin American contexts, we will not be able to develop and apply indigenous models of church planting and theological training.

Fourthly, church discipline and doctrinal standardisation. In Latin America, many churches that call themselves evangelical are doctrinally outside the standards of historic Christianity. At best they preach a prosperity gospel, and in several cases they are cults disguised as evangelical churches. A healthy association of churches promotes a visible expression of those marks of the true gospel in a way that isolated and detached churches cannot achieve. Churches involved in money laundering and the drug trade are sadly not isolated cases in Latin America. Cases of corruption among pastors and churches abound. A healthy association of churches promotes objective and verifiable standards of discipline by expelling those churches that fall into a pattern of extortion.

Fifthly, independence from western resources. Many Baptist churches still depend on financial and leadership resources from western churches. Unlike continental Europe, the geography of Latin America means it has been historically difficult for its people to integrate. But now, the possibility for integration between churches in the Andes or in coastal regions has never been greater. Perhaps the most effective way to locate and train qualified leaders for the next generation, give guidance and planning in church planting, and unite in missionary efforts, is through an association of churches. If this is not done, the ties of dependency of the Latin American church to the west will continue for generations to come, most especially among Baptists, whose reliance on the west is stronger than among other denominations.

LDC: The presence of Baptists in Italy dates back to the unification of the country in 1861 and the end of the Pontifical State in 1870. The first missionaries from the British Baptist Mission Society (Clark and Wall, 1863) and the US Southern Baptist Convention (Cote, 1870) were characterised by an admirable evangelistic zeal but a lack of theological depth. In 1884 they merged into a single entity, joining forces in confronting such a huge task.[4] While Charles Spurgeon warned British Baptists about the dangers of liberalism, and the early fundamentalist movement in the US encouraged evangelicals to defend the core tenets of the biblical gospel, Baptist missionaries in Italy did not give churches a theological awareness other than the basics to survive in a hostile culture dominated by Roman Catholicism. On the whole, they had an indifferent attitude towards the need for theological clarity in the controversies of their generation.

It is no surprise then, that when the Baptist Evangelical Christian Union of Italy was eventually formed in 1956, it soon identified with the liberal and ecumenical wing of Protestantism. Its association to the World Council of Churches (1977), the Barthian re-drafting of its Statement of Faith (1990), the covenant with the liberally-minded Waldensian and Methodist churches (1990), and the ever-increasing alignment to theological liberalism in doctrine and ethics were only consequences of that programmatic choice.[5]

Another stream of Baptist presence, this one 'evangelical', began in the late-1940s around the city of Naples. The US-based Conservative Baptist Foreign Mission Society (now WorldVenture) sent missionaries to plant churches in that area, along with a publishing house and children activities. In the context of these missionary endeavours, the publication of Spurgeon's Catechism in Italian needs to be noticed.[6] These general Baptist churches (with five local congregations) formed as association in 1972 (Assemblea Evangelica Battista in Italia, or AEBI) that continues to this day.

A significant event that spearheaded the growth of the reformed Baptist presence was the publication of the Second London Confession of Faith (1689) by the theological journal of the Istituto di Formazione Evangelica e Documentazione (IFED) in Padova

– Studi di teologia – on the occasion of the confession's third centenary (1989). For the first time, the most important confessional document of reformed Baptists was made available in Italian.[7] Interest in reformed theology was also promoted by the pioneering work of Italian theologian Pietro Bolognesi[8] and encouraged since the 1990s by the circulation of works by the Puritans, Old Princetonians, and present-day authors such as J.I. Packer, Walt Chantry, John Piper, and Mark Dever.[9] Since 1988, IFED has been providing resources (such as *Studi di teologia*, annual theological conferences, preachers' workshops) and training opportunities that have formed a generation of readers and church leaders who have become friendly towards reformed theology.

The combination of these factors created the context for a reformed Baptist presence that moved beyond a generic interest in reformed theology. A first attempt in this direction came with Associazione Chiese Evangeliche Riformate in Italia in 2002, a network of churches in Sicily closely associated with the European Missionary Fellowship (EMF). Despite its good intentions, ACERI never took off and was short-lived. Other churches and missionary initiatives, though mildly referring to a reformed identity, continued to operate within independency and through para-church connections such as missionary conferences.

Other local churches began to adopt the Second London Confession of Faith (1689) and to shape congregational life according to reformed Baptist principles. These churches began to develop a network of like-minded pastors and congregations. In 2006, the Evangelical Reformed Baptist Churches in Italy (Chiese Evangeliche Riformate Battiste in Italia, or CERBI) convened in Bologna to form the first and only association of reformed Baptist churches in the country.[10] CERBI was founded and eventually joined by churches which had gone through a journey of doctrinal and ecclesiological reformation from Brethren, Pentecostal, and independent backgrounds. Usually the steps included coming to an appreciation of reformed theology, drawing closer to like-minded churches going through the same process, adopting the 1689 Confession of Faith, and re-directing church life according to confessional parameters.

As happens in all transitions, the path was not free from controversy and struggle, but there was a determination to offer Italy a reformed Baptist association of churches that would nurture internal fellowship among the members and build a platform for co-operative efforts for the sake of the progress of gospel work. One of the entrenched patterns of Italian culture is its rampant individualism under the formal respect of a distant authority. Reflecting this cultural trend, gospel work (even missionary work) has often suffered from fragmentation and isolationist tendencies. The possibility of forming a confessional association in the context of Baptist congregationalism was a new and promising development.

What are the essential elements for the successful formation of an association of churches?

LDC: So far, CERBI as an association of reformed Baptist churches is an example of a healthy, stable, and forward-looking association. It therefore provides a useful example of what it means to have a successful association in a minority context. CERBI was launched by six churches in 2006, and is now, in 2021, made up of thirteen churches. CERBI is not a denomination as such, given the fact that congregationalism is its ecclesiological framework. While respecting the importance of local churches, CERBI bonds them together on a confessional basis and creates the context for co-operation on commonly agreed projects.[11] While other churches maintain an interest in reformed theology which does not translate into subscribing to any historical reformed confession or in associating with other churches, CERBI is a unique example of the possibility for confessional churches to operate within a congregationalist framework while taking advantage of the strength of doing things together. In CERBI's ecclesiological understanding, this perspective is called 'congregationalism of communion'.[12]

CERBI seeks to develop common ministries between churches, especially for pastors (e.g. annual fraternals or 'company of elders') and church members (e.g. the annual conference and celebration: the so called 'agape' which is held on 25 April each year). The structure of the fellowship is maintained as 'light' as possible: a commission of three pastors (elected every three years) is in charge of decisions made by the company of elders, and another commission of three pastors is responsible to evaluate their work and report to the company of elders.

In 2015 CERBI drafted a Programmatic Statement which reads:

The Evangelical Reformed Baptist Churches in Italy are:

- Rooted in Scripture, Word of God, in accord with the classical reformed faith;

- Allied in an ecclesial network for mutual support and growth;

- Committed to assimilate, proclaim, and apply the gospel of Jesus Christ in every area of life;

- Projected towards the extension of the kingdom of God through the conversion of sinners, Christian discipleship, and spiritual, social and cultural renewal until the Lord comes.

In the Italian context where strongholds of Roman Catholicism and secular trends of thought prevail, evangelicals must develop their witness to have a deep and large vision. This is why CERBI churches try to encourage all Italian evangelicals to have an identity that is rooted in Scripture and in the rich history of the faithful church. Through supporting the work of IFED, their desire is to impact non-reformed evangelicals to develop a faithful and robust evangelical faith as well as allowing liberal and Roman Catholic circles to deal with the evangelical faith, something that they have not been doing so far.

CERBI is also dedicated to the encouragement of church planting projects and the common witness of churches in Italy. Since its foundation, several church planting projects were launched: Breccia di Roma (2010); Rovereto (2011); Milano (2012); Breccia di Roma San Paolo (2018); Verona (2020). This indicates the importance of association to church planting, and is particularly important in minority contexts that are generally characterised by small and scattered congregations.

JDC: While associations of churches were an integral part of the formation of Baptist churches in North America during the nineteenth century,[13] this pattern was not replicated by their peers in Latin America.[14] D. A. Carson mentions that one of the consequences of the growth of secularism in the west is a reluctance to form any kind of accountable associations.[15] The formation of associations of churches is always connected with the exercise of authority. This partly explains why it is more difficult to form associations of churches in the west today. The challenge of forming successful church fellowships today is even greater than it was two hundred years ago when Andrew Fuller was part of the Northamptonshire Baptist Church Fellowship.[16]

I propose three elements that, given our particular Latin American context, are essential for the formation of an association of churches: a common history, a common organisation, and a common vision.

Firstly, a common history: looking to the past. A sense of identity and belonging can only be achieved when the same past is shared, when people are part of the same historical narrative. When you have the same heroes of the faith and central figures of an ecclesiastical tradition in common, then a sense of common identity is formed. Belonging to the same historical narrative gives meaning to ethical values, both individually and ecclesiastically, and is essential for the long-term permanence of any association of churches. One of the most important elements in achieving this is sharing a common confession of faith, which not only gives a sense of current but also historical permanence. The creation of the Second London Baptist Confession of Faith responded to this need for historical belonging to the universal church, connecting Baptists to other Protestant traditions but at the same time distinguishing them. The use of a common confession of faith was one of the distinguishing marks of early Baptists in the seventeenth century.[17]

This element is difficult to achieve in a Latin American context because we lack a common history, the vast majority of our churches were founded within the past forty years. It is imperative to adopt a historic confession of faith as a foundational basis, and to expand it on controversial issues of the day, such as matters of marriage, gender, and sexuality. I would argue that adopting a historic confession of faith for the purpose of forming an association is far better than the creation of a new confession that lacks the historic affiliation and sense of unity that an older confession provides.

Secondly, a common organisation: looking to the present. A local church at its very essence is an association of believers.[18] An association of churches should be based on some of the principles of the local church as an association of believers, but extend them to a macro level, bearing in mind that associations of churches are not churches in themselves.[19] I would like to give an example of how this works in practice. I have worked in many churches in the highlands, jungle, and suburban areas of Peru where groups of churches worked together in co-ordinated activities, church planting, and missionary endeavours. In practice they were associations of churches, even though they were not united by a confession of faith, nor did they have a common history. What was it that united them? The same ecclesiastical practice. The style of congregational worship, the evangelistic methods, the version of the Bible (among others things) were common elements in these churches and served as the basis for their functioning in unity. In practice, it was easier for two churches of different confessions of faith to work together if they shared these common elements, than for two churches with the same doctrinal confession, but with a different ecclesiastical culture.

Writing towards the end of the nineteenth century, Charles Hodge said that one of the most essential elements for the formation of an association of churches is geographical proximity.[20] However, I believe this presupposes a time when culture and geographical space were two intimately linked concepts. In other words, the advent of the Internet has caused the natural formation of church networks to be based not on geographical proximity, but on cultural proximity. Thus, in the UK, a church in London and a church in Birmingham may seem to have more in common with each other than one in a small village just outside of either city. An association of churches must be acutely aware of these factors, and be as broad or as narrow as it wishes to be in its inclusion of different denominations, cultures, and, yes, subcultures. In practice, the breadth or narrowness of an association is perhaps the most fundamental factor in why one church joins a particular network of churches and not another. In other words, a healthy association of churches should have principles that reflect the ecclesiastical convictions of the network of churches, and avoid, in the inclusion of the confession of faith, points related to the particular cultural idiosyncrasies of each church, such as the musical instruments used, or the translation of Scripture employed. An association of churches derives principles from the local church, but it is not a local church.

Thirdly, a common vision: looking to the future. The vision of the association of churches will be determined by its leadership. The selection of leaders should not be random, but driven by what needs to be achieved. In times of constant change, mature and older leadership will provide assurance and a secure anchor. In times of stagnation, more innovative leadership will bring about change more quickly. Above all, leadership must be able to project a vision of the future rooted in the past, but with practical and direct applications in the present.

It must be able to project beyond the difficulties of the moment, and sustain a long-term vision. Millard Erickson defines three essential tasks of leadership in a partnership of churches: a common purpose, discipline among the churches, and united efforts.[21] Erickson writes that a partnership of churches takes place, 'when churches enter into an organisational alliance to achieve their common purposes. They come together in what is called a council or association of churches. It is essentially a co-operative fellowship of denominations, each of which retains its own identity.'[22]

What would happen if we fail to establish strong associations of churches?

JDC: I would like to give three possible consequences of failing to have strong associations of churches in the context of Peru, and Latin America more broadly.

Firstly, churches are endangered. The church in the west is often unaware of how much its culture, society, and politics are built on the Christian values of tolerance, freedom of speech, right to private property, and more beside. This is not the case in much of the developing world, where social values have Christian elements to a much lesser extent. But with increasing secularisation, there may come a time when the civil liberties we have taken for granted are lost, and tolerance of Christianity will end. In such an event, churches will respond in four different ways, as they have done throughout its history: they will suffer persecution, some will deny core elements of Christian belief and behaviour, they will meet in secret, or they will migrate elsewhere. The government agenda against evangelical Christianity in Latin America is one or two generations behind that in Europe. The only way to secure legal representation, and to be able to continue to enjoy constitutional rights that favour the preaching of the gospel and the flourishing of common grace in society is through a collective representation of the church in associations of churches. I fear that unless strong associations of churches are established in this generation, the next generation will suffer greatly.

Secondly, churches are ill-equipped. Much of the church in Latin America has depended on its western brothers for financial resources and leadership for its institutions, creating an unhealthy cycle of paternalism. Our churches lack their own financial resources. The best way to increase our ability to organise resources for the purpose of planting new churches, founding new seminaries of high theological quality, and doing efficient mission work on an independent basis is through the formation of an association of churches. Unless this can be achieved, it will be difficult for the Latin church to develop its own leadership capable of responding to its own context, and to take leadership of its own theological institutions, churches, and missions.

Thirdly, churches are socially ineffective. If anything distinguishes the church in Latin America, it is its emphasis on the Holy Spirit as the agent of social change through the church. This social change has taken two main forms in the Latin American context: liberation theology and integral mission. Liberation theology was developed by the Peruvian Gustavo Gutiérrez in the early 1970s in Roman Catholic circles. Integral mission was developed by theologians such as the Ecuadorian Rene Padilla in the mid-1980s. Both approaches sought the political influence of the church, and were influenced to varying degrees by left-wing political systems – in the case of Liberation theology, even by Marxism.

The development of a robust Latin American political theology must take place in the context of the church, and be rooted in the historical roots of orthodox Christianity. The application of any public theology through the church in a society is directly related to the macro-level organisation of that church. In the case of independent churches in Latin America, the implementation of any public theology effectively can only happen in the context of effective administration through associations of churches, under the regulating normative of a historic confession of faith. Unless this is the channel through which our public theology flows, the union between Marxism and the evangelical church will continue to be a reality in Latin America.

LDC: Italy is a mission field, and an association of reformed Baptist churches should think hard about ways to implement healthy partnerships between local churches and mission agencies or individual missionaries. CERBI made extended efforts to elaborate guidelines for such relationships. The document that resulted, 'Co-Workers in God's Field: On The Relationship Between Churches and Missionaries/Missionary Agencies (2018)', summarises well some important ecclesiological and missiological points.[23] Here only some points of the document will be highlighted.

'Co-workers in God's field' (1 Cor. 3:9) is the way the apostle Paul describes the network of different subjects, all belonging to the universal church, who are active in the work of God. In line with biblical teaching, churches sometimes commission specific ambassadors for services to support the evangelisation and building of the church itself. Within the network of churches, these people are sent to support the work of the church (Phil. 2:25), to plant new churches (Acts 13:2-3), and to provide various services (Acts 11:30; 12:25; 15:30). Within these movements there is sufficient flexibility, not harnessed in rigid institutional paths, but also an accentuated sense of belonging to the one church, and the need for reporting, that is, sharing paths of service. Over the course of history, these light structures connecting sending churches and receiving churches have been called 'Missions' or 'Missionary Agencies'. Missions are therefore para-ecclesial agencies that connect churches and groups of churches within the universal church and facilitate obeying the Lord's mandate to make disciples.

In recent history and contemporary church experience, these agencies have become the protagonists of the mission, showing a considerable ability to operate that tends to be independent of, or unrelated to, the life of the churches. Meanwhile local churches have gradually become more introspective, localised, and not always able to cultivate a missionary vision worthy of the name. The role of local churches and associations having diminished, that of missions agencies has grown, often reversing the burden of responsibility and the roles of each.

With the reversal of roles in the reality of the contemporary evangelical church, too often the relationships between churches and 'Missions' has also been reversed, with the latter becoming the central focus of initiatives and churches becoming, if they were not already, subjects that are basically passive. This has created evident ecclesiological imbalances with heavy and negative consequences on the overall structure of the church. What took place was not collaboration but replacement; not synergy, but autonomy; not partnership, but competition, or mutual indifference. To remedy this, the Lausanne Covenant (1974) has opportunely invited everyone to rethink the relationship between churches and missionary agencies in the spirit of collaboration in the gospel, 'We urge the development of regional and functional co-operation for the furtherance of the Church's mission, for strategic planning, for mutual encouragement, and for the sharing of resources and experience.'[24]

It is evident that the 'Mission' as a para-ecclesial agency is called to assist the church or local churches in a spirit of circular sharing of gifts and collaboration in the promotion of God's work. On the other hand, the church or churches must reappropriate their role in God's plan, without delegating the mission to others while they themselves are not directly committed to it or take unhelpfully submissive attitudes. The relationship, therefore, must be rebalanced so as to reconstruct a primary responsibility upon churches in carrying out the divine mandate and the subsidiary function of the para-ecclesial agencies in supporting that work.

Each of our churches has had or has sporadic and/or ongoing collaborations in the field with missionary agencies and/or missionaries. There are varying experiences, from stories of co-existence marked by mutual indifference or mistrust, to fruitful intersections characterised by organic integration. In Italy, in general, biblically healthy models of relationship have not always been established. This is, on the one hand, because of a prevailing ecclesiology marked by unstable local identities and precarious church conditions and, on the other, by a general spirit of independence and disinterest in the local context on the part of foreign missions or missionaries. This is not in itself sufficient motive to nurture feelings of scepticism toward possible future collaborative developments. On the contrary, it is our task to work to re-establish relationships on healthy terms as far as the biblical framework is concerned, while also being responsible so far as the missiological responsibility is concerned. This requires the commitment to biblically review structures inherited from the past, both by churches needing to mature their missionary vision, and by missionary agencies and/or missionaries whose task it is to enrich the life and witness of the church and not to work in a self-referential way. The presence of missionary agencies and missionaries is a precious resource for the life of the church, and the evangelisation and planting of new churches. Our desire is to be an active part in the process of mutual fertilisation aimed at the expansion of the kingdom of God in Italy.

To join together in practical ministries of service, evangelism, prayer, institutional representations on behalf of evangelicals, or support for religious freedom, the Evangelical Alliance Statement of Faith provides a sufficient level of doctrinal agreement. However, the planting of churches and the ministry of the church, in the church, requires a more stringent doctrinal agreement, in our case based on the Second London Confession of Faith (1689). It is unthinkable to associate in planting new churches or to share the responsibilities of conducting those churches unless we have mutually embraced a shared confessional ecclesiology that distinguishes our confessional churches.

Conclusion

In this chapter we have provided an overview of the need, viability, and urgency of church partnerships in our respective contexts. There are similarities between the situations in Italy and Latin America:

- Recent Baptist origins. Both in Italy and Latin America, Baptist influence began in the late nineteenth century, mostly due to the influence of foreign missionaries, primarily from North America and Great Britain. However, while growth in Italy has been uniform, growth in Latin America has been exponential, especially from the 1970s onwards.
- Minority presence. In both Italy and Latin America, reformed Baptists are a minority in

their respective contexts. The characteristics of church associations in both contexts are doctrinally similar, especially in their emphasis on public subscription to the Second London Baptist Confession of Faith (1689) as a bond of historical unity and identity. Both contexts see subscription to a historic confession of faith as essential.

There are also points of difference:

- Different obstacles in forming associations of churches. The Italian culture is more individualistic than Latin American culture, which creates difficulties in seeking union between churches. Latin American culture has a colonial background that is different from Italian culture, and has inherited more denominational quarrels from its parents.
- The Italian context is more secular than the Latin American context, and with better national government structures. In the Latin American context, the development of an association of churches will also serve to better protect the benefits for pastors.

Despite these differences, Italian and Latin American Baptist churches are aware, in light of their history and present context, that forming associations of churches is fundamental for the sound and healthy future development of the Lord's church.

May the Lord bless each of our respective churches as we seek to be more effective, and work for his glory.

Notes

1. One of the most representative cases of this is the Aymara tribe, with a population of just over 2 million. The tribe is separated into two parts with Lake Titicaca in the centre. One half is in Peru, the other in Bolivia. They are one ethnic group with a common history, language, and culture, but as a consequence of an arbitrary foreign division they are divided into separate countries. This is not to say that the dreadful deeds of the European settlers were worse than those of the native inhabitants. The myth of the 'noble savage' popularised by Rousseau is just that, a myth devoid of historical veracity.
2. Timothy Keller, *Center Church: Doing Balanced, Gospel-Centered Ministry in Your City* (Zondervan, 2012), p. 361.
3. Lyle Schaller, *44 Questions for Church Planters* (Abingdon, 1991), p. 12.
4. See, D. Maselli, *Storia dei battisti italiani 1873–1923* (Claudiana, 2003).
5. A sympathetic history of the Italian Baptist Union is given by M. Ibarra Pérez, *Costruire la comunione. I primi 60 anni dell'Unione Cristiana Evangelica Battista d'Italia, 1956-2016* (GBU, 2016).

6. C.H. Spurgeon, *Un catechismo* (Centro Biblico, 1966).
7. 'La confessione di fede battista del 1689', *Studi di teologia* NS I (1989/2) N. 2.
8. The Festschrift on the occasion of his seventieth birthday gives an idea of his significant impact on Italian evangelical theology. See 'Il coraggio della verità. Studi in onore di Pietro Bolognesi in occasione del suo 70° compleanno', *Studi di teologia* NS XXVIII (2016/2) N. 56. Particularly relevant for reformed Baptist ecclesiology are his books *Il popolo dei discepoli. Contributi per un'ecclesiologia evangelica* (Alfa & Omega, 2002) and 'Elementi di ecclesiologia', *Studi di teologia* NS XXIV (2012/2) N. 48.
9. Through Italian publishers such as Alfa & Omega, Passaggio, Coram Deo, BE Edizioni, and others, scores of reformed books have been produced.
10. 'Italy: Reformation starts again', *Evangelicals Now* (June 2006), p. 9; 'Italy', *Evangelical Times* (June 2006) p. 9.
11. P. Patuelli, 'An Update from Italy', *Reformation Today* n. 267 (2015) pp. 23–5.
12. 'The ecclesiology of communion is a lived experience of inter-ecclesial relations which recognises that, biblically speaking, the life of the local church must establish relations of communion with other local churches based on the common confession of the evangelical faith and aimed at supporting the work of the gospel, in the various territories in which they are located' (Company of Elders 1/2014). See *London Confession of Faith* (1689), art. 26.7; 26,14–5.
13. Gregory A. Wills, 'Who Are the True Baptists? The Conservative Resurgence and the Influence of Moderate Views of Baptist Identity', *Southern Baptist Journal of Theology*, Vol. 9.1 (2005). p. 33.
14. William Cathcart, ed., *The Baptist Encyclopedia* (Louis H. Everts, 1881), p. 47.

15. D.A. Carson, *Christ and Culture Revisited* (Eerdmans, 2008), p. 132.
16. Andrew Fuller, 'State of the Baptist Churches in Northamptonshire (1814)', *The Complete Works of Andrew Fuller*, ed. Joseph Belcher, Vol. 3 (Sprinkle Publications, 1988), p. 481.
17. Philip Schaff, *The Creeds of Christendom, with a History and Critical Notes: The Evangelical Protestant Creeds, with Translations*, Vol. 3 (Harper & Brothers, 1882), p. 738.
18. James Bannerman, *The Church of Christ: A Treatise on the Nature, Powers, Ordinances, Discipline, and Government of the Christian Church*, Vol. 1 (T&T Clark, 1868), p. 87.
19. Edmund P. Clowney, 'The Church', in *Contours of Christian Theology*, ed. Gerald Bray (IVP, 1995), p. 111.
20. Charles Hodge, *The Church and its Polity* (Thomas Nelson and Sons, 1879), p. 92. I am aware that Hodge writes from a Presbyterian perspective, as does Bannerman in *The Church of Christ* referenced earlier. However, the principles outlined by both for the operation of presbyteries have many applications for the independent context. Independents would benefit greatly from studying the work of Hodge and Bannerman.
21. Millard J. Erickson, *Christian Theology* (Baker, 1998), p. 1142.
22. Erickson, *Christian Theology*, p. 1142.
23. <https://www.cerbi.it/Chiesa_missione2018_ENG.pdf> (accessed 6 August 2021).
24. On the contribution of the Lausanne Movement to this discussion, see also the *Lausanne Occasional Paper*, n. 24 'Cooperating in world evangelization: a handbook on church/para-church relationship', (1983) <www.lausanne.org/content/lop/lop-24> (accessed 6 August 2021).

6

Maintaining Strong Associations

John Benton

'There are some things which big churches can do which small churches can't.' That's true. But a friend rightly responded to that comment by saying, 'Actually there is nothing a big church can do which small churches can't do in association with each other.' Point made.

Associations are good for churches of all sizes. It is not healthy for large churches to become isolated and behave as if they are self-sufficient. However, most churches are relatively small and need to know that they are not second best (Rev. 3:8). And it is often associations, which under God, empower small churches and make them resilient and effective for Christ's kingdom.

Inter-church relations in the New Testament

As we have already seen in this volume, the churches of New Testament times worked together – even at a distance. Their fellowship was fostered by the apostles and was expressed in a number of different ways. These included:

- Greetings shared between the churches, with individuals named, in the apostolic letters (Rom. 16:1-16; 1 Cor. 16:19-20; Phil. 4:22).
- Churches in the same geographical region being mentioned together in apostolic letters (1 Cor. 16:19) and sometimes addressed together (Rev. 2 – 3).
- Churches sharing the apostolic letters with each other (Col. 4:16).
- People circulating around the fellowships – even apart from the apostles, it is clear that early Christians, teachers and prophets moved among the churches on the Lord's business (Acts 11:27; Rom. 16:1-2; 1 Cor. 16:12).
- Offering hospitality to Christians from other

churches who were on their way through (Heb. 13:2; 3 Jn. 5-8).
- Organising collections for churches to help other churches who were suffering and in need (Acts 11:29-30; 1 Cor. 16:1-4; 2 Cor. 8:3).
- Churches together supporting the mission of the apostles both financially and by sending personnel (Phil. 4:15; Acts 16:1-3).
- Churches sometimes sharing Christian workers (Col. 4:12-13).
- Communicating news of the churches between the different congregations (Eph. 6:21-22; 1 Pet. 5:9).
- Encouraging churches to pray for work in other churches, especially where there were opportunities for the gospel (1 Cor. 16:9; Col. 4:3).

Although all the early churches were linked across the Mediterranean world of the first century, given the comparative slowness of travel in those days, it is reasonable to think that churches in the same geographical region would have given particular support to one another and worked together.

Indeed Acts 9:31 can speak of 'the church throughout

Judea, Galilee and Samaria' enjoying a time of peace and growth. There were obviously separate and independent congregations in this area and we should not think of a regional church, but the closeness of association between the different churches does seem to be inferred by Luke's willingness to use the singular term 'church' for this group.[1] There fellowship appears to be a close fellowship.

But how does a group of churches build and maintain healthy, neighbourly relationships?

Three keys to healthy association

What are the biblical principles which can guide us as to how to make and maintain good relationships with one another as churches? This overlaps with the general question about what makes for good relationships between people or families or other bodies. But good church relations do have their own particular requirements.

The central necessities can be summed up under the three words: confession, communication and care. We confess the same Lord Jesus. We take interest in and communicate with one another across the churches. We express practical care and help for our sister churches.

Thus, confession, communication and care are to be mutual. So we add that adjective to our headings.

Mutual confession

The basic Christian confession of faith is 'Jesus Christ is Lord' (Phil. 2:11). Demonstrated by his resurrection from the grave and exaltation in heaven, we rejoice in this truth together.

But, of course, that marvellous declaration has to be carefully defined and defended according to Scripture in order for our faith to be sound and kept free from heresy. Who is Jesus? Why did he die? What does it mean that he rose again? How is he the Lord of the church? How does he build his church? For a healthy association, the churches must agree together on what God's Word teaches about such things. They must believe the same truths about Christ and how his churches are to function. Christ is the head of the church and our sure foundation. This is expressed and celebrated by the churches adopting a biblical confession of faith which is agreed between them.

In the New Testament, the apostles embodied and defined the truth of the gospel. But even there we find various fragments of 'doctrinal statements' embedded in what seem to be hymns quoted in Paul's letters. We think immediately of Philippians 2:6-11 which sets out the truth of the person of Christ in his humiliation and exaltation. Again, Colossians 1:15-20 comes to mind, where Christ's supremacy both over this world and the world to come is declared. Similarly there are the 'faithful sayings' of a doctrinal and practical nature in Paul's pastoral epistles, e.g., 1 Timothy 1:15; 3:16; 2 Timothy 2:11-13. These hymns and faithful sayings were probably a simple way of teaching the truth in a memorable way to the congregations.

Jude, the half-brother of our Lord Jesus Christ, was able to speak of the need to 'contend for the faith that was once for all entrusted to God's holy people' (v. 3). So let us not be hesitant about doctrinal statements which seek to summarise biblical teaching. A healthy association stands together doctrinally.

Mutual communication

This, of course, is fundamental to any relationship. And it is a two-way process. If friends don't talk we know that the relationship is either very superficial or that something has gone wrong between them. If communication is all one way something is amiss. A thriving relationship will be indicated by the fact that we take interest in, and want to know how, each other are doing. Paul was so desperate to know how things were going in the newly planted church in Thessalonica that he sent Timothy to find out (1 Thes. 3:1-2). We too should want to know how the Lord's work is prospering in other places.

There are different levels or depths of communication. In the early church letters were exchanged (1 Cor. 7:1). Sometimes emissaries were sent who reported back (Acts 14:27; 1 Thes. 4:6). But best of all there were face to face meetings which enabled the fullest and clearest communication (Acts 20:38; 2 Jn. 12; 3 Jn. 14). The apostle John connects face to face meetings with complete joy. Face to face hopefully means no misunderstandings.

We live in a much busier world than that of the early church. We so often find ourselves saying 'I haven't got time.' This is one of the great challenges which stands in the way of associations of church functioning properly in the contemporary world and we will return to this later.

Mutual care

Healthy relationships ultimately spring from loving hearts. It is very moving to read what Paul writes to the

Philippians, 'I have you in my heart ... God can testify how I long for all of you with the affection of Christ Jesus' (Phil. 1:7–8). He cared about them.

But it was not just the apostles who declared such care for the churches. When Paul or Peter were writing their letters, quite often, members of the church where they were presently located asked if their own greeting could be included to those in the recipient church (Phil. 4:22; 1 Pet. 5:13). Greetings were sent back and forward in mutual care. Brothers and sisters in other places mattered to the early Christians.

A true camaraderie had been fostered between the congregations – even distant ones – and that, as we have already noted, overflowed into practical care. People wanted to help out others. The more well-off Gentile congregations expressed their love for the poorer churches in Judea by sending financial help (Rom. 15:26). Care was shown by hospitality (Heb. 13:2). And especially the early churches were called to remember those who were suffering persecution (Heb. 13:3).

Bringing these fundamentals into focus we can see that mutual confession, mutual communication, and mutual care give us the keys which make for a healthy and strong association of churches.

Being practical, the depth and strength of relationship between the churches will to a large extent depend on pastors and elders being pro-association and active in promoting the mutual life of an association. Our leaders set the tone in every area of church life. If church leaders are enthusiastic and willing to give time and energy to the association, on top of their local responsibilities, it will kindle a belief in their congregation that other churches matter and we are all on the same team.

It falls to pastors and those 'at the front' in church to most naturally share news from other congregations and encourage interest in things like association meetings. Where a pastor obviously values the association and with a smile on his face speaks of his friends within the association and the benefits of the association, pretty soon others in the church will catch the vision. They will get a taste of the fact that, though their first commitment and love is rightly to their own local church, it is also a breath of fresh air to have their horizons widened and to take interest in what is going on elsewhere.

Ten threats to association

What are the issues which undermine associations of churches? What tends to make people think that associations are not worth bothering with?

There is one problem which always lurks in the background. One of the great characteristics of twenty-first-century life is lack of time. The old days of the Saturday association meetings with a speaker, where folk from different churches got together three or four times a year and chatted together afterwards over a tea and a bun, are long gone. We now seem always under pressure.

Having visited Kenya on a number of occasions I can remember some of our poorer African brothers and sisters commenting on the frenetic pace at which we westerners tend to live compared with their more relaxed way of doing things. Their joke with us was, 'You have the watches, but we have the time!' How very true! We may be materially rich, but we are 'time poor'.

Association among the churches is good. What are some of the difficulties that tend to undermine it? Here are ten problems on which to reflect.

Loss of priorities

Why are we time poor? A major reason is that we try to do too much. The emergence of digital technology is a factor in this. Computers and the Internet make it possible to do more than ever and so squeezes our available time more than ever before. Because we can do more we feel we must do more. Because so many resources are available on websites, and via TV and email, and because we can access social media at almost any time, the whole world, from the concerns about climate change to the latest light-hearted entertainment, clamours for our attention. We tend to be very distracted people always trying to fit more into our itinerary – more work, more good causes, more leisure activities.

Association with others takes time. If we are going to foster a healthy and worthwhile fellowship of churches it will need to take priority over other things. We must think it through, see we have a responsibility to the wider church, and for the glory of Christ step away from less needful activities, and give slots in our diaries to association.

Feeling overburdened

Among the other background factors which tend to undermine association is also the culture of looking upon ourselves as fragile people who mustn't take on too much. Obviously there is sense in not overdoing things. This can lead to burn out. But many of us seem to have been trained to set the bar too low for ourselves. We wrap ourselves in cotton wool. We too readily declare ourselves to be overburdened and often it is involvement with the association which is the first activity to be downgraded or axed from the schedule.

Actually most of us are not as fragile as we think we are. We are not bone-china teacups which easily smash when dropped. We are more like plastic cups which bounce. Human beings need some stress.[2] Just as muscles in our body rapidly deteriorate if they are not used, so if we coddle ourselves too much we make ourselves weaker than we could be. When it comes to association, some of us need to beware laziness (Prov. 6:6).

Lack of openness

Information is power. Sometimes information has to be withheld from others for reasons of data protection and to uphold confidentiality. But there are some characters who love to withhold information from others as a way of saying, 'I'm more important than you are.' They love to play the childish game of, 'I know something that you don't.'

An association of churches should work at being

as open as is possible in all its dealings (2 Cor. 4:2). Otherwise it will be in danger of alienating those who are not 'in the know'. There will inevitably arise an 'in group' and an 'out group' which is bound to lead to tensions within the association. This very much erodes trust and undermines cohesiveness.

Party spirit

To belong to a good association of churches is very beneficial but, because we are naturally proud and sinful, this can easily become tribal (1 Cor 1:12). People and leaders of a group of churches can draw together (which is good) but do so in a way that can incline towards becoming cliquish or even the disparaging of others who are not 'one of us'.

We have joined the association because we believe that the churches that belong to it have taken their stand together in the right place. But that can so easily spill over into a less than loving spirit towards other churches, even other gospel churches. 'They are not sound!' we proudly declare. But can't we disagree with other Bible believing churches who are clear on the fundamentals without being derogatory of them? If we can't do that we have a great deal to learn spiritually. Where such a party spirit emerges it is very ugly and puts people off getting involved in an association. Christians don't like priggishness, they don't like 'empire building' – at least they shouldn't. What is needed is an association which is clear but generous at the same time.

Bad communication

We have said that mutual communication is vital for fellowship. But where communication breaks down, fellowship is threatened. People get left out. Sometimes adopting new digital packages may feel very up to date and efficient, but if it means that various people who don't have that software or couldn't use it comfortably even if they did, are side-lined then it damages rather than helps the association (1 Cor. 14:9). Those people will feel like their voice doesn't count.

Again where there is no proper system of feedback to those who administer the workings of the association, it will feel as if they do not really want to hear from people. They want to run the association rather than serve the association. We owe it to other human beings, made in the image of God, that they should know they have been heard. An association, like every Christian, needs to be quick to listen (James 1:19).

Bad organisation

An association requires organisation. The very nature of creation breathes design with the purpose of efficiency. God is a God of order (1 Cor. 14:33). In God's church, 'everything should be done in a fitting and orderly way' (1 Cor. 14:40).

Some people are very good at organisation. Indeed the apostle Paul was able to speak of those who have a spiritual gift of leading and governing diligently (Rom. 12:8). An association needs to have an organisational structure and to put in place those with proven abilities in administration. Of course those people must be accountable to the association, but their good work should be recognised and honoured.

Where everything is last minute and runs continually on the brink of being a shambles, the God of order is missing and we should not be surprised that association becomes a burden rather than a blessing. We will come back to this matter later in the chapter.

Busy churches

Sometimes, when the Lord graciously brings a church success in its ministry, everything becomes very busy. The preaching ministry makes a real impact and many people are drawn to the Sunday meetings. There are many more people looking for pastoral care. There are newly converted people to look after. There are unlooked for avenues of outreach into the community. New works among children, or mothers or older people, begin to open up and beg for personnel and attention. With such joyous encouragements happening at the local level it is easy for the association to be forgotten.

But that is very discouraging for those churches which are not seeing the same level of blessing. 'The successful church is too good for the likes of us,' others might easily say. Maybe the pastor of the busy church can't give so much time to the association. But he should find some time. And perhaps he could ask a deacon or an elder to take particular interest in the association on behalf of the church.

Dominant characters

Sadly there are some men who never learn to be team players. They feel they must always have the limelight – or at least dominate a group. Whatever is decided must be done their way or they pull out or start criticising. They have never learned to argue their case humbly, and they have never learned to work with others who do things slightly differently. Either they are the captain and centre forward of the team or they take their ball home and won't play. It's childish behaviour, but that is how some men, even some gifted pastors, are.

These characters ruin associations. No opinion counts except their opinion. This undermines the fellowship. People and churches do not want to join an association simply to be dictated to by 'Mr Always-Right'.

Young pastors

Beginning the ministry is a daunting experience. Having left Bible college or some assistantship where not too much is expected of them – suddenly they are thrown in at the deep end. They have to produce two sermons every Sunday and lead the midweek meeting – or at least provide material for the small groups. Suddenly they find that they are not dealing with pastoral issues in textbooks, but in the lives of real people – some angry, some broken – sitting in their front room. The demands seem incessant. It can be a baptism of fire which consumes a young pastor. And involvement with the association, understandably, might get put on the back burner.

A good association will be there, from the beginning to

provide a safety net and help for young pastors in those early years. Then, instead of forgetting the association, they will be thankful for it and be drawn into it.

Lack of teaching on association

Churches will not take much interest in an association unless they see, from Scripture, its necessity and its value. Biblical teaching on churches associating together needs to be spelt out from the pulpit clearly and winsomely and ought to be part of any membership course which a local church may run for those who are joining.

There is a great emphasis in the New Testament on the unity of all God's people (Jn. 17:20-21). There are also many warnings concerning false teachers and compromised churches (Mt. 7:15-23). In an association of churches we make the first step beyond the local congregation towards that wider, Holy Spirit inspired, oneness which the Lord so desires.

Three essential association builders

We have seen some principles of association regarding mutual confession, communication and care. We have also noted a number of attitudes and actions which threaten the health of an association of churches. But what can we do to build up the group of churches as a viable association?

It should be said that associations need to capitalise on the use of digital technology where possible. During the recent pandemic and consequent lockdown, churches were unable to meet in person. But we held together through learning to use applications like Zoom and YouTube in order to stay in touch and communicate. These methods can never replace the essential and joyful experience of worshipping together in one location. But they have their place and we should utilise their potential in communicating together as associations. We have already mentioned how time poor we are as a society. Well, meeting on Zoom does save all that time spent in travel to get to committee meetings. Saving time like this may well enable more pastors to take more interest in the associations and engage more. We still need in person meetings, especially for an AGM and perhaps other times of fellowship, but a balance could be struck between personal and digital interaction which would prove highly beneficial.

That being said, what should we focus on in order to grow and build up an association? What should we continually have our eye on? There are three essentials: agreed procedures, practical assistance and inspirational fellowship.

Agreed procedures

The purpose of an association is to help one another as churches to the glory of God. The general guidelines of the way we come together and relate to each other need to be agreed by all the churches and be made clear and explicit. Then we all know our 'rights and responsibilities'. This comes back to being well organised.

What are the doctrinal standards of the association? What are the requirements for a church to be a member of the association? How is the administration side of the association to be handled? How are people to be appointed to those administrative posts? Are those posts to be salaried and if so how are they to be paid for and who sets the level of pay? To whom are those in the administration accountable and how are the churches involved in that accountability? How can churches, pastors and ordinary church members make their views known at an association level? What are the procedures if a church begins to drift from the doctrinal position adopted by the association? Should the association seek charitable status or is that out of place given current trends in society? How should the association meet together? How is the administration of the association to remain the servant of the churches rather than becoming a master? Are there any other groups of evangelicals which the association should relate to and how?

These and many similar questions need to be answered to everyone's mutual satisfaction. And, once agreed, the association needs to adhere to those procedures. Leaders or committees who ignore the rules will give an air of arrogance and flouting accountability which will be detrimental. And if, because of some unforeseen emergency, something different has to be done by those administering the association, the reasons for that need are to be quickly and helpfully explained. There is a need for good communication in such circumstances.

Of particular importance in our contemporary context is the matter of safeguarding issues related to the churches. Sadly, power can be misused. When people in leadership in a local church abuse others, not only may the civil authorities need to be called in if a serious offence has been committed, but the association of churches ought to be informed and be in a position to help. At present many churches refer to para-church ministries which are independent. These organisations can be professional and very helpful. However, often they have no real ecclesiastical accountability themselves and their work can proceed in such a way as to override the God-given authority of the local church (Mt. 18:15-20). Ideally, having learned from others and yet with a biblical mindset, the association should be the avenue through which such a situation is dealt with. This needs to be both just and sympathetic as it advises the people of the local church what they should do while the kingdom authority of the local congregation is upheld. It is imperative that, for coming years, a fair and open procedure be agreed and adopted for such situations. Where these are dealt with maturely and with proper care, attention and justice for victims, it will turn evil into good, or at least make the best of a bad job. This will build confidence in an association.

Practical assistance

Churches need to see the practical benefit in being involved in an association. This should be evident at a number of different levels.

First, there is the pastor to pastor level. Pastors in an association should not regard one another as rivals but as brothers, seeking to assist one another. There is benefit from meeting pastors from a broad spectrum within biblical evangelicalism. But meeting with the church leaders of your own local association ought to be especially helpful and precious. We come from the same church polity. We are part of the same team. We understand each other's challenges more keenly. We can benefit from the different gifts of different pastors and swap pulpits from time to time knowing that the preacher will confirm the congregation in its beliefs and churchmanship without causing difficulties. Younger pastors can benefit from the years of experience of older men in ministry. Beyond this, friendship may well spring up between ministry families within the association. Pastors' wives will find special understanding and support from other pastors' wives. Such practical assistance fosters the 'ties that bind' across the fellowship of churches.

Second, there is the congregation to congregation level of support. At different times, the various churches will have different needs and go through various phases of spiritual prosperity and attendance at their services. If one congregation is planning a fellowship day somewhere, in order that as many as possible can participate, perhaps a nearby congregation could provide a day of activities for the children so that mums and dads can join in with the fellowship. If some churches are going through a difficult time of decline it might be good if a larger congregation could set up a rota so that three or four people from their own congregation go along on Sunday mornings to the smaller church. This is not to try to take over, but simply to lend support and just give the message, 'You matter and we are here for you.' Again this level of help will encourage the various congregations to see that the association is worthwhile and at the same time individual Christians from different churches will get to know and love one another, which is always a good thing.

Third, there is the administration to congregation level of support. This is a magnificent help, especially to smaller churches. Not every church possesses expertise in many areas of vital importance. The central administration of the association may be able to provide things like payroll services for a smaller congregation. There may be financial help by way of loans or gifts to which the administration can direct churches. Legal advice concerning data protection, buildings, terms and conditions of a pastors' work and much more is of immense help. Again, such practical matters are likely to become increasingly necessary in coming years as the society in which we live becomes increasingly hostile to biblical Christianity and the ethical standards it has a duty to try to uphold. We need help from one another in difficult times. Paul speaks of 'striving together as one man for the faith of the gospel without being frightened in any way by those who oppose you' (Phil. 1:27–28). Such fellowship will be of inestimable value.

Inspirational fellowship

If an association is going to be built and congregations become enthusiastic about it, then it needs to provide benefits of real quality.

An 'anything will do' and 'cheap as chips' approach to what the association does will not enhance but actually have a very negative effect on the heart of an association. It will not encourage time-poor church members, for example, to give up a precious Saturday with the family to get to an association meeting.

Christians of a certain generation had a very scrimping attitude to money. 'Nothing should be lavish, always look for the lowest cost, because we need to save our money for the Lord's work.' When it comes to our personal lives that kind of attitude has a lot to commend it. But let me enlighten you. The local church is the Lord's work. Missionary endeavour is the Lord's work. And the association is also the Lord's work. And we are not to have an 'anything will do' and 'cheap as chips' attitude to the Lord's work. We are to give of our best to his work. We can hear the words of King David echoing in our ears as he looked to build the temple, 'No, I insist on paying for it. I will not sacrifice to the LORD my God burnt offerings that cost me nothing' (2 Sam. 24:24).

When associations do things together look for the best speakers who are really going to help people and who people want to hear. Look for comfortable venues with good facilities. They don't need to be luxurious but please avoid what is spartan, dingy and uninviting. Look for venues which are easily accessible even to folk who, geographically, might live at the outer limits of the association. Do not go for a venue which is simply convenient for the administration. These are the Lord's people we are seeking to encourage.

And as we have said, the association should be a vehicle through which churches communicate with each other for prayer and encouragement. When the opportunity for this occurs we must try to make those messages interesting and specific. Prayer requests like 'pray for the Lord's blessing on the preaching' or 'pray for our Christmas outreach' or 'pray for those who are unwell' are so bland that they could have been written by anyone at almost any time. When Paul communicates he takes opportunity to name names, 'Pray for pastor Archippus to be given strength to continue his valuable ministry' (cf. Col. 4:17). Wherever possible we need to take one another more into each other's confidence in our requests. Be clear in what you are seeking to do in your Christmas outreach. Give some times and dates and name who is speaking. If someone is being baptised we might not be able to give names, but perhaps we can say something like 'a young woman who has grown up in the church', or 'a neighbour of one of our members who has come to the Lord'. Seek to spark imagination. Imagination ignites prayer.

Of course, a certain amount of administration has to be addressed at AGMs and the like. But it is good to find creative ways of getting the essentials across in the most engaging way. Let us never make the work of the Lord and of his churches look boring and unappetising.

With this in mind it is also good for the association to be aware of gifted people in the churches who are not just the pastors. Perhaps there are ethical issues which would be good to air at an association and there are medical professionals or lawyers in the churches who could give very insightful talks. Perhaps there are those in the churches who are particularly gifted musically, or by way of catering whose involvement would greatly enhance an association fellowship day.

Maybe some of the items I have suggested will cost quite a lot of money. But it will be worth it. If the people of the churches find that such fellowship really does encourage and inspire their faith they will be prepared to pay.

Going to meetings of the association should not be a chore, but an exciting prospect. It should be a chance in enjoy one another's company, celebrate the great Lord Jesus we serve, and affirm 'this is us' and 'I'm so glad to be here!'

Notes

1. See, Jonathan Leeman, *One Assembly*, Appendix 2 (Crossway, 2020), p. 143.
2. See, Jonanthan Haidt and Greg Lukianoff, *The Coddling of the American Mind* (Penguin, 2018), p. 23.

Conclusion

Andrew King

This book has made the biblical, theological, and practical case for church associations in general and described some specific historical examples. I am so thankful for the work each of these brothers have put into their chapters to help stimulate our collective thinking, planning, and actions for associations in the future. Most of the book has described the history and activities of the Association of Grace Baptist Churches (South East). God has been very gracious in holding this particular Association together through the many changing scenes of life over the last 150 years. Indeed, this anniversary year, which has prompted the writing of this book, is testimony to God's kindness and sustaining grace. Praise God!

Whilst certainly painting no panacea, the authors have shown that more has been done together when an association of churches has shared the same gospel purpose and ecclesiology, than had these churches remained isolated and overly independent. Chapter one argued that there is no biblical basis for a church to isolate itself from others of the same doctrinal basis. Rather there is a strong biblical case for local church interdependency. And although formally organised associations are not explicitly identified in Scripture, there is a good biblical case to encourage them. Just as the practices of formal local church membership is described and explained but not explicitly named, so too is the practice of organised inter-church co-operation. That is what associations do!

But when we say the 'Association' what exactly do we mean? Within our South East Association, the word correctly means two different but connected things. One meaning is 'the network of sixty-six independent churches working together in gospel ministry' and the other is 'the charity and Committee that employ staff to serve these sixty-six churches with administrative and financial support'. Whilst that serves as a good basic distinction, some activities fall somewhere in between, such as when the Association secretary is invited to give churches pastoral support or help in the search for new pastoral appointments. However, the distinction shows that the South East Association charity exists to serve the South East Association of churches.

But the authors in this book have also shown that all associations, and especially formal associations, must continually review and revise things to prevent stagnation and drift. The watchword 'semper reformanda' – always reforming – is necessary for associations too. So, what might we consider doing to help our South East Association become healthier and more useful in the years ahead?

In their excellent book on the nature of church ministry, *The Trellis and the Vine*, Colin Marshall and Tony Payne make a vital distinction between the necessary supporting trellis and the vine that the trellis serves. In a healthy church, the focus will be on the vine work of making more disciple-making disciples to the glory of God. Pretty much everything else should be classified as supporting trellis work. Our church buildings, our finances, even our weekly programme of activities are all trellises that support the core work of gathering the saints to worship God and equipping the saints for ministry. And this understanding – that trellis work only exists to support vine work – must also remain clear and central to every association of churches. We need to restate that the core purpose of this and any association is to help and support individual churches in their gospel mission: preaching the gospel and making disciples of Jesus Christ.

Chapter two describes the activities of some early Baptist associations in England. These comprised a small number of churches often located in just one geographical county. Chapter three however describes how our Association has grown over the past 150 years from a small number of closely located churches in central London to a larger number spread over the wider geographical area of the South East of England. And while the number of churches has increased over the years, the individual size has sadly declined. Whilst the core mission purpose of our Association has not changed, a larger spread of smaller churches has led to changes in our organisation, communication, and decision-making processes.

In addition to these size and geographic changes, government administrative and legal requirements have significantly increased over the last 150 years. This explains why the charity side of our Association has grown in order to serve the churches with more financial, legal, and administrative support. We should be thankful for common grace provisions that keep buildings safe and protect against fraud and various forms of abuse, but these government requirements can take up a high proportion of a smaller church's resources and, with a larger charity made up of many smaller churches, there is always a risk that this works against our biblical conviction of independency and moves our focus to maintain trellises rather than grow the vine.

So, what actions might we take to ensure our Association churches and charity keep focussed on supporting churches on the vine work of gospel mission? What actions might we take to ensure local churches remain healthily independent rather than become over reliant on the charity? Here are four that I consider worthy of priority:

1. Arguably the most strategic action is to develop a scheme to train and mentor more new pastors/elders and supplement the training and support for existing

ones.[1] This is because – in almost all cases – as go the pastors, so goes the church. That should hardly surprise us as one of the key roles of pastors is to lead! Therefore, our Association will surely be stronger and healthier if more of our churches are led by teams of pastors/elders with a clear focus on vine work. If pastors prioritise the gospel ministry of Christ-exalting all-of-life, nook-and-cranny relational discipleship, then so eventually will the rest of the church. And Association pastors who lead their churches wisely will in turn help foster warm and generous relationships with sister churches. Such pastors will also equip their members to serve responsibly and so minimise the risk of overdependence on the charity.

However, if men come into leadership without good training and a positive experience of Grace Baptist ecclesiology and Association life, it will prove harder to keep our churches united and working well together. Pastors without Grace Baptist theological convictions in their hearts are more likely to lead their churches away from our shared Association principles. And, of course, regardless of their ecclesiological convictions, pastors without godly character and skill in shepherding a diversity of people are likely to act as reverse magnets, repelling people and leading to decline. As go the pastors, so goes the church.

As two of the objects of the Association charity are to 'uphold and promote the Doctrinal basis' and to 'promote the unity of its member Churches' I believe there is a strong case for the charity to deploy some of its time and money into a renewed strategy to support and help facilitate Association churches in the training of future leaders. This is key: the charity should not train men, the churches should. But the charity can serve the churches with the necessary trellis work needed to enable such training. Key to this strategy must be the provision of both theological training and a healthy church experience (for example through apprenticeship schemes). New pastors need both the theological conviction to keep a clear direction of leadership and the pastoral wisdom to discern the wisest speed of change. Much of that is learned by experience.

To this end, some initial discussions with our friends at London Seminary have explored the potential of a partnership for a four-year Pastoral Apprenticeship Scheme in addition to our current pastoral training grants scheme. The new scheme would likely include the following elements:

- London Seminary: our churches currently send men to London Seminary, and we have good relationships with its leaders. Trainees would either study part-time over four years or full-time over two years, followed by a two-year assistantship role in one of the training churches.
- Training churches: a small number of Association churches would need to make a long-term commitment to invest some of their own time and money in training men. Such churches will need to function rather like teaching hospitals, with an expectation of trainees being involved in the routine life of the church before moving on elsewhere. The Association charity would provide a proportion of the trellis support through finance and housing for trainees.
- Trainee pastors: such men would need to become full members of their training church and start with the intention to serve later in another Association church. The decision to accept and then keep each trainee would remain with the training church.
- Scheme administration: the scheme would need

> structure (in terms of an assessed programme of activity) and management (in terms of advertising, recruitment and co-ordination). This would be another way the Association charity would provide trellis support.

Some of our churches sadly have no pastors or elders; some need additional men to join those already serving, and quite a number have men nearing retirement. Without strong local pastoral leadership our churches will not flourish in the longer term. Please pray that the Lord will help our Association charity and churches to work well in partnership to train many new pastors and elders. Above all, please pray that the Lord will raise up suitable men to train.

2. Another connected action must be to train up new and existing deacons in each of our churches to take the biblical responsibility of local trellis work.[2] Whilst the short-term 'contracting-out' is a great help to a church plant or revitalisation, in the longer-term leaving deacon work to the Association charity can become harmful. Local deacon trellis work builds better ownership of decisions and responsibility in each local church which then better binds together the shared

corporate life of each church. However, if too much work or decision making remains with the charity, this runs the risk of a church either not taking their own full responsibility for independent church life or resenting external limitations from the Association charity (which are often ultimately government requirements).

Too often pastors and elders are left to do deacon work. This both diverts them from their ministry of prayer and the Word and, if they lack the skills – which sometimes they do – can lead to poor decision making and management of the church's assets.

We need to train both pastors and deacons to keep our Association of churches healthy and independent. And when local deacons own their own trellis work this also avoids overburdening the charity staff who are available to support all of our sixty-six (and, in the future, hopefully more) Association churches. One way to facilitate this is through local deacons and pastors networking together more effectively. More association between deacons (and musicians, Sunday school teachers, and others that play a key role in church life) ought to be an organic and more manageable way to train and support across our churches.

3. A further action will be to review how we continue to promote and communicate the shared activities and ministries of our churches, especially to younger generations in our new digital age. We need to think of fresh ways of ensuring that the shared activities and ministries of the Association churches are equally communicated as well as the governance work of our charity. We need to find ways of better collecting and then communicating and sharing news about joint evangelistic endeavours, youth conferences, pulpit swaps, fraternals, new pastoral appointments, training days, and district prayer meetings. This is not an easy thing to do, of course, and requires people to have the necessary skills and creativity, especially in the use of print and visual media.

Perhaps another way we can draw new people into Association life is by better signaling that our annual gathering has always been more than just a charity AGM: the afternoons have always included some news of the vine work of shared ministry. In future we should follow the approach our friends at Grace Baptist Mission have taken where the charity AGM takes place in parallel with other events. Our annual day needs to be promoted as more about the vine than the trellis.

One partnership I hope will develop further is with Grace Publications Trust, with whom I also serve. Martin Luther is well remembered for using both the pulpit and the press to promote biblical truth, and this is something we should also copy. I hope this partnership with a Grace Baptist publisher will also help us write and circulate more books on ecclesiology to serve our UK context as well as developing the capability to produce video and online media in the future.

4. Another way to strengthen the unity between our Association churches will be the launch of an annual spring pastors' overnight conference to both facilitate better networking and provide a forum for deeper theological and practical discussion regarding our Association.

As was helpfully made clear in chapter one, Baptists hold firmly to the principle of the independence of the local church. The Association charity committee is not a church court, and the Association secretary is certainly not a bishop. But as an association of churches, we do need good and clear ways of communicating and discussing a variety of theological and organisational matters. Chapter three records that for many years until 1980 the Association held two annual meetings (the spring AGM and autumn half yearly meeting). For some time in the more recent past there was also an annual fellowship away day for pastors and their wives.

Currently the two Association forums for discussion are the Committee (comprised of elected representatives from the churches and charity staff) and the AGM. One of the reasons for launching this new annual pastors' meeting will be to provide an additional forum for more considered theological discussion about our Association life together. Each year we hope to gather our pastors/elders at a conference centre and enjoy food and fellowship. But as well as this, we hope to prepare and then discuss a number of papers on various theological, cultural and practical matters that relate to our Association. In this way, the opportunity for our church leaders to gather and study should better inform the working of the Committee and the annual Association Day/AGM. The Association charity will take the lead with the organisational and financial trellis work for these gatherings.

This book has been about associations. They can be a great blessing to churches to provide mutual support and encouragement. But if a Christ-exalting, true gospel-preaching church is in our area but not in our Association (or in another network) we should not allow our Association walls to limit our co-operation and fellowship. As J.C. Ryle famously said: keep hedges low so that you can shake hands over them.

This book has specifically been about the Association of Grace Baptist Churches (South East). This particular Association continues to be a great support to many churches, especially in encouraging a clear and confident Grace Baptist ecclesiology that clarifies the boundaries of each church and therefore safeguards the gospel.

But most of all this book has been about honouring Jesus and his glorious gospel of saving grace. Why else do our churches gather if not to glorify him and lift him up to others? Why else do our churches associate together if not to partner in this same gospel work of preaching Jesus Christ?

Whilst I commend our Association life to you and would encourage more churches to join or form new associations, my primary aim is to commend Jesus Christ. To him be eternal glory.

Notes

1. The New Testament clearly teaches a plurality of elders in each local church. Although some churches distinguish the full-time paid elder with the title 'pastor' I tend to use the titles interchangeably as all elders do pastoral work. Where I serve, I am one of two co-pastors. The key thing to grasp is the need for a plurality of men.
2. An excellent recent book on this is, Matt Smethurst, *Deacons: How to serve and strengthen the church* (9Marks, 2021).

Contributors

James M. Renihan is president of IRBS Theological Seminary, Mansfield, Texas.

Ryan King is pastor of Grace Baptist Church Wood Green and leads the Grace Baptists in Europe team of Grace Baptist Partnership. He is married to Uliana.

Robert Strivens is pastor of Bradford on Avon Baptist Church. He was previously Principal of London Seminary and continues to lecture there in church history.

Greg Tarr is currently training for pastoral ministry at Southern Seminary in Louisville, Kentucky. Originally from London, Greg spent some of his formative years at a Baptist church in Guildford while working as a software developer. He is now a member of Third Avenue Baptist in Louisville, but with a desire to return to the UK to serve as a pastor. Outside of his studies, Greg enjoys outdoor activities such as running, mountain biking and skiing.

Paul Smith is married with four children and he is a full-time elder of Grace Baptist Church in Broadstairs, Kent. After studying history in Cambridge, he spent over ten years teaching in secondary schools.

Nigel Hoad is married to Lucy and is a father of three with eight grandchildren. Now recently retired, Nigel qualified as a Chartered Quantity Surveyor and worked in private practice and has served in leadership roles in several churches. In recent years Nigel became full-time in Christian ministry and served as Director of Home Mission for the AGBC(SE).

Barry King is a pastor of Dunstable Baptist Church and leads the Grace Baptist Partnership.

Leonardo De Chirico (PhD, King's College, London) is pastor of the Reformed Baptist Church in Breccia di Roma and Lecturer in Historical Theology at the Istituto di Formazione Evangelica e Documentazione (IFED) in Padova. He blogs on Vatican and Roman Catholic issues from an evangelical perspective at VaticanFiles.org. He is also Director of the Reformanda Initiative and co-host of the Reformanda Initiative Podcast, and is author of several books, including *Evangelical Theological Perspectives on post-Vatican II Roman Catholicism* (2003), *A Christian's Pocket Guide to the Papacy* (2015), *A Christian's Pocket Guide to Mary* (2017), and *Same Words, Different Worlds: Do Roman Catholics and evangelicals believe the same gospel?* (2021)

Jaime D. Caballero (ThM, Westminster Theological Seminary) was born in Lima, Peru and is married to Ellie. They currently live in Cork, Ireland where he serves at Douglas Baptist Church. He is commencing doctoral studies in John Own and English Puritanism.

John Benton trained in science, but ended up as a pastor in Guildford for thirty-six years and was editor of the monthly newspaper *Evangelicals Now*. He is married to Ann, they have four married children and John is at present 'pastoring pastors' as Director of Pastoral Support for the Pastors' Academy based at London Seminary.

Andrew King is married to Lena and they have two daughters. He has been a pastor at Highbury Baptist Church since 2011 and now also serves as the Association Secretary for AGBC(SE).